The Six-Minute Solution:
A Reading Fluency Program

Gail N. Adams, M.Ed.
Sheron M. Brown, M.A., M.S.

Grades 3-8 and
Remedial High School

Copyright © 2004 by Sopris West.
All rights reserved.

Permission is granted to the purchasing teacher to photocopy the *Practice Passages, Automatic Word Lists,* and the reproducible forms in the *Appendix* for use in his or her classroom only. No other part of this work may be reproduced or transmitted in any form or by any means, electronic or mechanical, including photocopying or recording, or by any information storage and retrieval system, without the express written permission of the publisher.

The *San Diego Quick Test of Sight Word Recognition* is copyrighted by the International Reading Association: LaPray, Margaret Helen and Ross, Ramon Royal. (January 1969). The graded word list: Quick gauge of reading ability. *Journal of Reading, 12,* 305–307. Reprinted with permission of the International Reading Association. All rights reserved.

ISBN 1-57035-919-9

Developmental edit by Claudia F. Manz
Copyedit by Francelia Sevin
Text layout by Edward Horcharik
Cover design by Edward Horcharik and Sebastian Pallini

06 05 04   6 5 4 3 2

Printed in the United States

Published and Distributed by

SOPRIS
WEST
EDUCATIONAL SERVICES
4093 Specialty Place ▪ Longmont, Colorado 80504 ▪ (303) 651-2829
www.sopriswest.com

Acknowledgments

We would like to express our appreciation to:

Dr. Anita Archer, the most gifted teacher we have ever known. Her inspiration, friendship, and encouragement were instrumental in the development of this book.

Dr. Susan Van Zant, our dear friend and colleague, for her willingness to assist us in writing some of the *Practice Passages* found in the *Six-Minute Solution*.

Judy Wollberg, Sopris West Program Director, whose support and guidance was invaluable to us throughout this project.

Anne Linehan, our colleague, dear friend, and supporter of our many endeavors.

Larry Adams, Jack Brown, and Jennifer Adams—our immediate family members—for their patience, understanding, and love.

Our mothers, Ruth Novelli and Joan Miscall, who first instilled in us the love of reading.

Gail N. Adams
Sheron M. Brown

About the Authors

Gail N. Adams is a veteran teacher with almost 30 years of experience in elementary and middle school. In addition to working as a resource specialist for the Poway Unified School District, Poway, California, Adams is an educational consultant for the San Diego Office of Education and the North County Professional Development Federation. As such, she was a contributing author and trainer for the materials developed under two California reading grants. Adams is also a nationally certified trainer for the *REWARDS* and *Summer Reading Camp* programs. She holds a Masters Degree in education with an emphasis in reading, and is certified in general education, special education learning disabilities, and as a reading specialist.

Sheron Brown has been an educator for 38 years. She began her teaching career in her home state of New Jersey, and has taught in Florida, Texas, Alaska, and California. She has been a classroom teacher for grades one through ten and an elementary administrator. Brown is a retired elementary reading specialist. She holds Masters Degrees in curriculum and instruction, reading, and educational administration. She has also been an educational consultant for the San Diego County Office of Education and the North County Professional Development Federation. Brown conducts workshops and teacher trainings for school districts and conferences throughout the United States and is the author of four books of word sorting and word study activities: *All Sorts of Sorts, All Sorts of Sorts 2, All Sorts of Sorts 3,* and *Words They Need to Know* (with Sally Oppy). All are published by Teaching Resource Center, San Diego, CA.

Contents

- 1   Introduction
- 5   Program Overview
- 7   Chapter 1: Assessment
- 13   Chapter 2: Selecting Fluency Partners and Instructional Groupings
- 17   Chapter 3: Training Students
- 25   Chapter 4: Student Progress and Record Keeping
- 31   Chapter 5: Comprehensive Strategies
- 35   Conclusion: More Than Six Minutes a Day
- 37   Practice Passages
    - 39   Level 1
    - 61   Level 2
    - 83   Level 3
    - 105   Level 4
    - 127   Level 5
    - 149   Level 6
    - 171   Level 7
    - 193   Level 8
- 215   Automatic Word Lists
- 241   Appendix
- 255   References

Introduction

Nothing is more painful and frustrating to a teacher than to hear a student arduously reading a sentence word by word, seeming to have to physically drag himself or herself to the end of the sentence. As educators, we have all heard students read in this manner time and again and have wanted to do something, anything, to help these disfluent students become good readers.

The *Six-Minute Solution* will help these students do just that. This research-based, highly effective instructional procedure for grades 3–8 (as well as remedial high school) builds reading fluency in only six minutes of the instructional day. Good readers as well as struggling readers benefit from the *Six-Minute Solution's* daily fluency practice. For an overview of the procedure, see *Table I.1*.

	Table I.1 AN OVERVIEW OF THE SIX-MINUTE SOLUTION	
Time	**Materials**	**Procedures**
1 minute	Timer 1 portfolio for each set of partners that contains: ■ 2 copies of the same *Practice Passage* in plastic sleeves. ■ 1 water-based ink pen and a damp sponge in a plastic bag. ■ 2 copies of the *Fluency Record*.	1. Announce that the fluency timings are to begin. 2. Partners retrieve their portfolios. 3. Partners record the date on their *Fluency Records*.
1 minute		1. Set the timer for 1 minute and say, "Begin." 2. Partner 1 reads first until the timer sounds. Partner 2 marks the errors and stopping point on his or her own copy of the *Practice Passage*.
1 minute		1. Partner 2 tells Partner 1 how many words were read, how many errors were made, and follows the error correction procedure. (See *Chapter 3, Days 1* and *2*.) 2. Partner 1 records the numbers on the *Fluency Record*. 3. Partner 2 wipes off the *Practice Passage* and gives the marking pen to Partner 1.
1 minute		1. Set the timer for 1 minute and say, "Begin." 2. Partner 2 reads the same *Practice Passage* to Partner 1 until the timer sounds. Partner 1 marks the errors and stopping point on his or her own copy of the *Practice Passage*.
1 minute		1. Partner 1 tells Partner 2 how many words were read, how many errors were made, and follows the error correction procedure. (See *Chapter 3, Days 1* and *2*.) 2. Partner 2 records the numbers on the *Fluency Record*. 3. Partner 1 wipes off the *Practice Passage* and returns the pen and sponge to the plastic bag.
1 minute		1. Students return their portfolios with *Practice Passages, Fluency Records,* and plastic bags to the designated place.

Struggling readers can gain fluency first at the word and then at the passage-level, while competent readers can be challenged to read more expressively using texts that are increasingly more difficult. Almost every student can benefit from fluency practice since, as they encounter more challenging texts, all students need to continue to grow as fluent readers.

Rereading to Build Fluency

As the saying goes, "practice makes perfect," whether it's shooting basketballs, playing the piano, or processing text in a smooth, efficient, and accurate manner. The benefits of repeated readings of the same passage have been well documented in many research studies. Rereading is recognized as an effective procedure to build reading fluency. The *Six-Minute Solution* helps students succeed at reading fluency using an instructional model that is based on repeated-reading research and partnering students whose instructional and fluency levels most closely match. Research supports the fact that students' reading skills improve when they work with peers in structured reading activities (Rosenshine and Meister, 1994; Greenwood, Delquadri, and Hall, 1989; and Stevens, Madden, Slavin, and Famish, 1987).

Partnering Students to Build Fluency

In the *Six-Minute Solution,* students' current instructional reading levels are determined, then they are placed in fluency partnerships. In these partnerships, one student reads the passage to his or her partner for one minute while the other student tracks the words read and errors made. The partners then switch roles. Each partner charts their own progress. The entire procedure takes only six minutes.

Decoding & Fluency

Experts may disagree as to what exactly is the best approach to teach students how to read, but they are in agreement as to what good reading "sounds" like. According to Carnine, Silbert, and Kameenui (1997), **fluency** is "reading smoothly, easily, and quickly." In order to read fluently, the reader must be able to decode the vast majority of words automatically at approximately 95-percent accuracy. However, although there is a clear link between fluency and decoding skills, fluency practice alone will not improve a student's decoding skills. Any underlying decoding problems must also be addressed either prior to or in conjunction with fluency practice.

Comprehension & Fluency

Research also shows a high correlation between comprehension and fluency. Reading comprehension suffers when students lack fluency. This is because, if students are not fluent, cognitive energies are focused on decoding and word recognition and therefore are not available for comprehension. In the words of Farstrup and Samuels (2002), **fluency** consists of "optical, perceptual, syntactic, and semantic cycles, each melting into the next as readers try to get meaning as efficiently as possible using minimal time and energy."

Independent Reading & Fluency

Fluent readers generally find reading to be a pleasurable activity. As a result, they read more. When the amount of time spent on independent reading increases, there are accompanying gains in reading-related skills. As students read more, they increase not only their comprehension, but also their vocabulary, background knowledge, decoding, and fluency skills. The "Matthew effect," a term coined by reading researcher Dr. Keith Stanovich, refers to the effect that in reading, as in other areas of life, "the rich get richer while the poor get poorer" (Stanovich, 1986).

Work Completion & Fluency

Fluent readers will be better able to complete both class assignments and homework. This is significant when you consider the amount of reading assigned to upper elementary, middle school, and high school students. As an example, Student A, a fluent reader, is able to read an average of 180 correct words per minute (cwpm). Student B, a struggling reader, has an average fluency rate of 60 cwpm. Both students are assigned the same amount of reading. Student A, with an appropriate fluency rate, is able to complete the assignment in two hours. Student B, who reads three times slower than Student A, needs six hours to complete the assignment.

Reading Achievement & Fluency Practice

Although the National Assessment of Educational Progress (Pinnell, Piluski, Wixson, Campbell, Gough, and Beatty, 1995) found that 44 percent of fourth-graders were not fluent readers, research shows that educators have the knowledge and tools to affect this problem. After analyzing many fluency studies, the National Reading Panel (National Institute of Child Health and Human Development, 2000) reported that fluency can be taught and that guided, repeated oral-reading procedures are "appropriate and valuable avenues for increasing reading fluency and overall reading achievement." Skilled readers read words quickly, correctly, and without hesitation. Students who have not become fluent readers continue to plod slowly through each sentence without experiencing the joy of quick, automatic, fluent reading. By its very nature, fluency practice supports comprehension. It provides a skill-building activity that enables students to move quickly through text. As students build fluency through rereading, they amass a larger reading vocabulary. As they begin to read with automaticity, their cognitive attention can be focused on the text's meaning instead of on word identification. The National Reading Panel found that repeated oral reading accompanied by feedback and guidance resulted in significant reading achievement.

The *Six-Minute Solution* uses both of these research-validated components (repeated readings of the same passage and oral feedback from peers) to build fluency.

Program Overview

The *Six-Minute Solution* is divided into the following sections:

>*Chapter 1: Assessment*
>*Chapter 2: Selecting Fluency Partners and Instructional Groupings*
>*Chapter 3: Training Students*
>*Chapter 4: Student Progress and Record Keeping*
>*Chapter 5: Comprehension Strategies*
>*Conclusion: More Than Six Minutes a Day*
>*Practice Passages & Automatic Word Lists*
>*Appendix.*

A description of each follows.

CHAPTER 1: Assessment
Assessment is critical in determining fluency partners and in selecting the appropriate reading level of the *Practice Passages*. *Chapter 1* provides step-by-step procedures for assessing your students' oral-reading fluency rates and instructional reading levels. It also includes the recommended oral reading fluency rates for students reading at each grade level.

CHAPTER 2: Selecting Fluency Partners and Instructional Groupings
Careful selection of fluency partners is important to the success of the *Six-Minute Solution*. *Chapter 2* describes the procedures for selecting partners based on assessment data, using either spreadsheet software or manual sorting. *Chapter 2* also offers suggestions for implementation in different grouping configurations—for entire classrooms, small groups, special needs classes, intervention programs, and cross-age tutoring programs.

CHAPTER 3: Training Students
Taking time to properly train students in the *Six-Minute Solution* procedures will ensure that the program runs smoothly. *Chapter 3* provides steps for introducing students to the concepts of fluency practice and cooperative partnerships. It also discusses how to teach students correct fluency partnership and management procedures.

CHAPTER 4: Student Progress and Record Keeping
It is essential to monitor student progress and make instructional decisions based on individual student progress. *Chapter 4* provides examples of how to interpret fluency data, adjust student reading goals accordingly, and support students who are not making adequate progress.

CHAPTER 5: Comprehension Strategies
Although the *Six-Minute Solution* is primarily a fluency-building program, the *Practice Passages* may also be used to instruct students in a variety of comprehension strategies. *Chapter 5* offers suggestions for teaching students how to summarize, paraphrase, retell, describe, sequence, compare, solve problems, and determine cause and effect.

Conclusion: More Than Six Minutes a Day

With the *Six-Minute Solution* fluency partnership model, students are able to increase their oral reading fluency by practicing for only six minutes a day on a regular basis. There will be times, however, when you will need to devote more than six minutes to fluency practice. The *Conclusion* outlines some of the situations you might encounter that will require extended fluency practice.

Practice Passages & Automatic Word Lists

This section consists of reproducible student *Practice Passages* (sets of nonfiction passages organized by readability levels from grades 1–8) and *Automatic Word Lists* (sets of the most-often encountered words in written English). The *Automatic Word Lists* are sets of 75 words.

The *Practice Passages* are organized by readability level, based on Flesch-Kincaid readability. Twenty passages are provided for each readability level for grades 1–8. The passages are all nonfiction informational passages that focus on science, social studies, history, and biographical topics. Nonfiction passages are used for two important reasons:

1. **Students who are struggling readers often lack general background knowledge about the topics in the *Practice Passages*.** All students benefit from fluency practice with passages from which they will gain information.
2. **It is easier to "hide" the readability level in nonfiction material.** To improve their fluency, students need to practice rereading passages at their instructional reading levels, which in many cases are below their chronological grade-level placements. A seventh-grade student who reads at the third-grade level may better accept reading an informational passage about sharks with a third-grade readability level than he would a narrative passage that seems "babyish."

The *Practice Passages* within each readability level are not thematic or dependent on one another.

The Appendix

The *Appendix* includes:

> *Fluency Assessment Report* (to be sent to families)
> *Initial Assessment Record* (to rank and match students)
> *Fluency Record* (for students to record their partners' progress)
> *Fluency Graphs 1, 2,* and *3* (an alternative method for students to chart their progress)
> *San Diego Quick Assessment of Reading Ability* (includes *Teacher Record* and student forms)
> *Three* Six-Minute Solution *Field Tests* (for readers who would like more information about the implementation and validation of the procedures included in this book).

Students may use either the *Fluency Record* or the *Fluency Graphs* for data collection. The *San Diego Quick Assessment of Reading Ability* may be used to determine students' instructional reading levels.

CHAPTER 1

Assessment

The first step in implementing the *Six-Minute Solution* is to determine students' instructional reading levels. This initial assessment will guide *Practice Passage* selection, provide data for selecting partners, and provide baseline information so that student growth can be evaluated. More specifically, the two-part assessment that follows (*Assessment 1* and *Assessment 2*) will determine:

- Students' oral fluency rates, i.e., correct words read per minute (cwpm) on a *Practice Passage* at their grade-level placements.
- Students' instructional reading levels (determined by either a group silent-reading test or the *San Diego Quick Assessment of Reading Ability* (in the *Appendix*). *Note:* If you already use an Informal Reading Inventory, you may use this data to determine students' instructional reading levels.

It is recommended that students be assessed for fluency three times a year (e.g., in September, January, and May) to ensure appropriate student progress and to validate that the partners are working well together and recording scores accurately.

It is always a good idea to keep families informed of children's fluency levels. The *Fluency Assessment Report* in the *Appendix* can be used for this purpose.

Students who have significant reading problems may need a more extensive assessment than is described in this program in order to determine the nature of their reading problems. This more extensive assessment information can either replace the *Six-Minute Solution* assessments or be used in conjunction with them. Use the assessment information you gather to guide you in addressing underlying deficits in skills, such as phonemic awareness and decoding. Instruction in these important skills may be conducted prior to or along with the implementation of the *Six-Minute Solution*.

Oral Reading Fluency

Materials
- One copy of a *Practice Passage* (from the *Practice Passages & Automatic Word Lists* section) at the students' grade-level placement, enclosed in a plastic sleeve or laminated. Each student in the class will read the same *Practice Passage* individually (e.g., one sixth-grade *Practice Passage* for a group of sixth-grade students).
- Copies of the same *Practice Passage* on which to record each student's stopping point and errors. Make the same number of copies as you have students.
- Digital timer or stopwatch.

Estimated Time
2.5 minutes per student.

Steps
1. Give the student the laminated copy of the grade-level *Practice Passage* and explain that the student is to read the passage aloud "quickly and carefully" until you tell him or her to stop. Record the student's errors and stopping point on your own copy of the passage as the student reads.
2. Set the timer for one minute and tell the student that the timer will begin when he or she starts reading.
3. Underline errors as the student reads. Mark a diagonal line when the timer sounds, indicating where the student stopped reading.
4. Thank the student and call for the next student. During the interval between students, count the number of errors and note the total number of words the student read. Subtract the number of errors from the total number of words read to determine the **correct words per minute (cwpm)**. Then prepare for the next student.
5. After all of the students have read the *Practice Passage*, record their scores.

Additional Fluency Assessment Tips
- Make sure the other students are not within hearing distance of the student reading so that they will not have prior knowledge of the *Practice Passage*.
- Count errors of proper nouns (such as surnames) only once.
- Do not count self-corrections as errors if self-corrections are made within three seconds.
- Do not count insertions as errors or as words read.
- Omissions are counted as errors.
- If a student reverses the order of words, count both words as errors.

Instructional Reading Level
Two types of assessments may be used to obtain a close approximation of a student's instructional reading level:

1. Word recognition, or
2. Group silent-reading test.

Although these two types of assessments may seem unrelated, because they both have an integral relationship with fluency, they are good informal indicators of a student's reading ability. It is not necessary to administer both a word recognition and a group silent-reading test.

The advantage of using a group silent-reading test is that it can be administered to all your students at the same time. While students are taking the test, you can read with individual students to obtain an oral-reading fluency rate. Word recognition tests are given to each student individually since students must read the words orally to you. Word recognition tests can be administered individually to students at the same time as the oral-reading fluency test (*Assessment 1*).

Word Recognition Test
Materials
- An assessment of a student's word-recognition level can be obtained with the *San Diego Quick Assessment of Reading Ability* (in the *Appendix*). Although this test is individually administered, it takes very little time per student.

Estimated Time
About 2 minutes per student.

Steps
1. Make copies of the *San Diego Quick Assessment of Reading Ability* student forms and *Teacher Record* (see *Appendix*).
2. Administer test as per the directions on the *Teacher Record*.

Silent Reading Test
Materials
- Copies of a silent reading test for all students in the class.

Estimated Time
Will vary, depending on test.

Steps
1. Choose a silent reading test that can be administered to the entire class during one class period. The selected silent reading test may be teacher-prepared or commercial. The important criteria is that the test yield a measurable score that can be used to rank students according to their instructional reading levels. Examples of commercially prepared tests which lend themselves well to this procedure include:

- Scholastic Reading Inventory (SRI) (Scholastic, 2003). Scores are reported in lexile levels.
- Gates MacGinitie (MacGinitie, MacGinitie, Maria, K., and Dreyer, 2003). Scores are reported in percentiles.
- McLeod Test of Reading Comprehension (McLeod, and McLeod, 1999). Scores are reported in grade levels.

2. Explain the test directions to your class and complete the practice items with the entire group.
3. Instruct students to begin working on the silent reading test. Be certain that students have something they can do independently when they finish the test.
4. After all of the students have finished, record their scores.

Appropriate Fluency Rate

A student's target **fluency rate** is based on the student's instructional reading level, *not* the current grade-level placement. For example, the initial goal for a sixth-grade student reading at a third-grade instructional level is 80–115 correct words per minute—the recommended oral-reading rate for third-grade readers. Once the student has met the initial goal, increase the **correct words per minute (cwpm)** goal to the upper range or move the student to *Practice Passages* at the next grade level. See *Table 1.1*.

Keep in mind that student partners always read the same *Practice Passage*. A fifth-grade English language learner (ELL) reading at a third-grade level may be partnered with a fifth-grade special education student also reading at the third-grade level. Occasionally, there may be an "outlying student" (one whose instructional reading level does not match that of any other student). An outlying student may need to be partnered with a teacher, an aide, or a classroom volunteer.

As a general rule, from fourth grade on, students should be reading a minimum of 100 cwpm in order to be able to fully comprehend what they are reading. Readers with fluency rates below 100 cwpm are spending most of their cognitive energy on decoding, leaving few resources to decipher context. Refer to *Table 1.1* for cwpm standards by grade level.

Note: Generally, students in the fourth grade or above who read below 100 cwpm need further formal or informal assessment of their decoding skills. Often students who have such difficulties need additional instruction in decoding.

Table 1.1 RECOMMENDED ORAL READING FLUENCY RATES	
Grade Level	Suggested Oral Reading Rate (cwpm)
1	40–60
2	50–95
3	80–115
4–5	120–150
6–8	150–180
9–12	180–200

Hasbrouck and Tindal, 1992. *For grade 1:* Shapiro, 1996.

Variation for Assessing Students in Special Needs Settings

Students who are enrolled in Title I, remedial reading, special education, or English language learner classes or who have significant reading problems may be more appropriately assessed using an individually administered reading test such as the Woodcock Reading Mastery Test (Woodcock, 2000). This test will help you determine instructional reading levels and gather information about underlying reading problems.

Assess remedial students using *Practice Passages* at their estimated reading levels rather than at their grade-level placements. Continue assessing to determine the level at which a student reads with 95 percent accuracy (i.e., five errors in a 100-word passage). This is the appropriate level for a student to begin building fluency.

Selecting Fluency Partners and Instructional Groupings

When selecting fluency partners, match students as closely as possible by both their oral-reading fluency rates and their instructional reading levels. An appropriate match is critical to success.

An example of an appropriate match is a partnership between two sixth-grade students whose instructional reading level is grade 3 and whose oral fluency rates are within ten words of each other. If one of these students had an oral-reading fluency rate of 85 cwpm and the other had an oral-reading fluency rate of 45 cwpm, these students would not be matched as fluency partners. The reason for this is that the student who has an oral fluency rate of 45 cwpm would not be able to follow along with his partner's more rapid rate of reading.

Keeping in mind that student partners must always read the same *Practice Passage,* you could partner a fifth-grade English language learner reading at the third-grade level with a fifth-grade special education student who is also reading at the third-grade level.

Occasionally, there may be an "outlying student" (one whose instructional reading level does not match that of any other student). This student may be partnered with a teacher, an aide, or a classroom volunteer.

Fluency partners can be selected by using spreadsheet software or by manually sorting students' oral-reading fluency and instructional reading-level scores.

Using Spreadsheets to Select Fluency Partners

For large groups of students, the easiest way to select fluency partners is to use spreadsheet software. The following steps will help you create the spreadsheet:

1. Begin by opening a new document (blank spreadsheet) and naming it (e.g., Language Arts Period 3, Mr. Smith's Third-Grade Class).
2. Label six columns with the following headings: last name, first name, date, grade, oral-reading fluency score (cwpm), and instructional reading level.
3. Enter data for each student.
4. Sort the data first by fluency (cwpm) and then by instructional reading level.
5. Assign fluency partners based on the sort. For example, the first two students on the list would be partners, the second two students would be partners, and so on.

Manually Sorting Scores to Select Fluency Partners

Another method you can use to select fluency partners is to manually rank students. The following steps will help you sort your students' scores more easily:

1. Sort your students' oral fluency scores from *Assessment 1* (see *Chapter 1*) in ascending order—from lowest to highest.
2. Sort your students' instructional reading-level scores (from the *San Diego Quick Assessment of Reading Ability* in the *Appendix* or on another reading test) in ascending order—from lowest to highest.
3. In the second column of the *Initial Assessment Record* (see *Appendix*), list students in the order of their oral-reading fluency scores.

4. In the third column of the *Initial Assessment Record*, list students in the order of their instructional reading levels.
5. Match students as closely as possible based on the data.

Selecting Instructional Groupings

The *Six-Minute Solution* is designed for an entire classroom, but the following grouping configurations may be used successfully:

- Entire classroom
- Small groups within a class
- Individual
- Special-needs classroom or group intervention
- Parent/student partnerships
- Cross-age partnerships.

Entire Classroom

In this instructional grouping, the entire classroom is assessed and fluency partnerships are assigned. All the Partner 1s read to their partners for one minute. While they are reading, the Partner 2s mark errors and stopping points on their own copies of the *Practice Passages*. The Partner 1s then record their final scores (cwpm) on their *Fluency Records*. All the Partner 2s then read for one minute. Results are tracked by the Partner 1s on their copies of the *Practice Passages*. The Partner 2s then record their final scores (cwpm) on their *Fluency Records*. The partners store their portfolios (containing the *Practice Passages, Fluency Records*, and plastic bag with pen and sponge). The fluency practice is over for the day.

Small Groups Within a Class

You may choose to assign fluency partners within small groups and call each small group to an assigned seating area for fluency practices. The group members can then also receive instruction from you in an area of the language arts curriculum. *Six-Minute* fluency practice may also be conducted in a "literature circle" or guided reading group before or after the partners read and discuss assigned books.

Individual

A teacher's aide or parent volunteer may be trained to conduct one-minute fluency timings with students who need extra practice.

Special-Needs Classroom or Group Intervention

Students who qualify for reading intervention programs should have reading-fluency as an instructional goal. These students may be placed in fluency partnerships based on assessment data and then trained in the *Six-Minute Solution* procedure (see *Chapter 3*).

Parent/Student Partnerships

Parents can be easily trained to conduct one-minute fluency timings and data recording either at the school or at home. Working with students on *Automatic Word Lists* and *Practice Passages* is a highly effective way families can support a school's readers. Home recording sheets can be brought to school and checked by you. Additional *Practice Passages* can be sent home based on the data. Parents will be able to have first-hand knowledge of their children's reading improvement on a daily basis as they conduct their children's daily fluency timings at home.

Cross-Age Partnerships

Many elementary schools pair older classes with primary classes in a "big buddy" setting. The older students conduct one-minute fluency timings and record the data of their younger "buddies." After the fluency timings have been conducted, the older students and younger students could then take part in whatever other "buddy" activities you have designed for them.

Training Students

Implementing the *Six-Minute Solution* to meet the needs of all students in a classroom can be challenging in terms of both management and instruction if you do not spend ample time training students in the procedures. Devote a minimum of two class-periods to training for a general education, upper-elementary, middle school, or high school class. It is most effective and efficient for students to begin reading a new *Practice Passage* on the first day of the week. Students then have consecutive practices before their final timings.

Students also need to be instructed in appropriate fluency partnership behavior (e.g., leaning in and whispering to their partners, remembering that the only person who needs to hear them are their partners, and providing appropriate corrective feedback on missed words). Addressing the classroom's noise level during training is the key to preventing many potential problems. Teachers are usually amazed at the low level of classroom noise when the fluency timings are in progress.

We also recommend that an explicit instructional model be employed when you are teaching the procedures. For example, introduce the procedure by modeling, then allow considerable guided-practice time (while you walk around giving feedback and remodeling as necessary) before students practice the procedure independently.

Taking the time to properly teach the *Six-Minute Solution* procedures will ensure that the program runs smoothly. Once students are properly trained, the entire fluency practice should take only six minutes of the reading period each day. Following are outlines for two days of training in the *Six-Minute Solution* procedures.

Day 1: Introducing the Fluency Practice

Materials
- One copy of a selected *Practice Passage,* enclosed in a plastic sleeve, for each student in the class.
- An overhead transparency of the same *Practice Passage* and a transparency marker.
- One zipper-lock plastic bag for each student that contains one small square of a dampened sponge and a water-based ink pen. (Alternatively, you can have every two students share a plastic bag of materials since the program only requires one plastic bag of materials for each fluency partnership.)
- Timer.

Estimated Time
20+ minutes.

Steps
1. Select the *Practice Passage.*
    - Select one *Practice Passage* to use for classroom demonstration and training. The readability of the selected passage should match the lowest level of reading in the class. For example, in a sixth-grade class, if the student who reads at the lowest level reads at the third-grade level, the passage selected for training should be at a third-grade readability level. It is important that students do not struggle while reading the *Practice Passage.*
2. Introduce the concept of fluency.
    - Introduce students to the value of building fluency, using language appropriate for their grade level. You may paraphrase the information provided in the *Introduction* and discuss the benefits of rereading, "practice makes perfect," the correlation between comprehension and fluency, and work completion and fluency.
3. Explain the *Practice Passages.*
    - Pass out copies of the selected *Practice Passage* to the class. Explain to students that the *Practice Passage* has numbers at the beginning of each line in order to help them keep track of how many words they read in one minute.
4. Model the reading fluency procedure.
    - Set the timer for one minute and demonstrate oral reading, using the overhead transparency of the *Practice Passage.*
    - Take care to model effective reading practices. With your pen, track as you read (without making marks) and underline unknown and incorrect words. Draw a diagonal line after the last word read when the timer sounds.
    - Continue using the transparency to demonstrate how to count the **total number of words read.** Write this number on the line at the bottom of the *Practice Passage.* To determine the total number of words read, use the line counts at the left-hand side of the *Practice Passage.* Starting at the number at the beginning of the last line read, simply count from that number to the last word read. This is the **total number of words read.**

- Now return to the beginning of the passage and count the number of underlined (incorrect) words. Subtract the number of underlined words from the total number of words read. Indicate that this is the total number of **correct words per minute (cwpm)**. Write this number on the line on the *Practice Passage:*

    Total Words Read _____
    − Errors _____
    = CWPM _____

5. Students whisper-read the *Practice Passage.*
    - Now it is the students' turn to read. Students "whisper-read" the passage, following the procedures of tracking, underlining unknown words, and drawing a diagonal line after the last word read when the timer sounds. Set the timer for one minute, reminding students to whisper-read. Say "Ready, begin" when you start the timer.
    - When the timer sounds, remind students to draw a diagonal line after the last word read. Ask students to figure out the total number of words read and write that number on the line on the *Practice Passage.*
    - Once students have written down the total number of words, ask them to determine the cwpm by counting any underlined words and subtracting this number from the total number of words read. If a student did not underline any words, then no words are subtracted from the total number of words read. Remind students to write these numbers on the lines provided on the *Practice Passage.* Walk around the room, carefully monitoring that students are reading and are determining their word counts.

6. Students reread the *Practice Passage.*
    - Inform students that they will now reread the *Practice Passage,* using the same procedure of whisper-reading.
    - When the timer sounds at the end of one minute, remind students to draw a diagonal line after the last word read and to follow the steps to determine the total number of words read and the cwpm. Once again, carefully monitor as students are reading.

7. Lead a group discussion about fluency practice.
    - Ask students to raise their hands if their cwpm was higher the second time. (The vast majority will have read more words the second time.) Now ask students to reflect on why they might have read more words the second time. Students may share their thoughts with a neighbor, within a cooperative group, or with the entire class. Sum up the discussion by noting that rereading the same passage helps people to become better readers.

Day 2: Introducing Student Partnerships and Fluency Practice Procedures

Materials
- One portfolio (folder with pockets) for each fluency partnership that contains two copies of one new preselected *Practice Passage* in a plastic sleeve, two copies of the *Fluency Record* or the appropriate *Fluency Graph* (see *Appendix*), and one plastic bag with sponge and water-based ink pen.
- One overhead transparency of the selected *Practice Passage* to be used as an example and one overhead transparency of the *Fluency Record* or appropriate *Fluency Graph*.

Estimated Time
20+ minutes.

Steps
1. Select a new *Practice Passage* at the readability level that matches the lowest reading level in the class.
2. Model the fluency partnership procedure.
   - Place the transparency of the *Practice Passage* on the overhead and ask for a student volunteer to be your fluency partner. Instruct the student partner to make some deliberate mistakes. Say to the class, "Watch me as my partner reads the *Practice Passage* to me. Notice what my pen is doing and how I am marking the errors. Notice also what my pen does when the timer sounds at the end of one minute." Set the timer and say, "Begin," to the reader. The student reads the *Practice Passage* aloud while you mark the reading errors. Draw a line after the last word read when the timer sounds. Ask the class "What did you observe me doing when my partner was reading the passage to me?" The most important behavior you want students to notice is how the pen "tracked" the words as the student was reading. Tracking helps students keep their place as they read and makes marking errors easier.
   - Once you have reviewed the procedure for marking errors and have noted the stopping point for the student, reverse roles in order to model the error-correction procedure. Remember to make a number of errors while reading so that the student fluency partner can mark them. The error-correction procedure is meant to be quick and to the point. See *Figure 3.1* for an example.
3. Model how to use the *Fluency Graph* or *Fluency Record*.
   - Using the overhead transparency of the *Practice Passage*, review how to figure out the cwpm by determining total number of words read and subtracting errors, for example:

                  Total Words Read   120
                           – Errors   5
                           = CWPM   115

> **Figure 3.1**
> **An Example of the Error-Correction Procedure**
>
> *While the reader is reading aloud for one minute, the fluency partner follows along and underlines any errors. When the timer sounds, the partner notes the last word read, then provides feedback in the following manner.*
>
> *Partner:* "You read _____ (total number of) words. You made _____ (number of) errors." The partner then points to each underlined (incorrect) word and pronounces it correctly for the reader.
>
> *Reader:* Records the cwpm on the *Fluency Graph*.
>
> *Note:* Establish a "No Arguing" rule between partners at this point in the training.

- Place a transparency of the appropriate *Fluency Graph* or the *Fluency Record* on the overhead (whichever your students will be using). Fill in the *date* and the *passage number,* then fill in the *cwpm.*
  Note: If you are using a *Fluency Graph* and this is the first time students have been introduced to recording on a graph, you may need to model graphing on subsequent days.
4. Discuss cooperative partnerships.
   - Be sure to make the point that students will work in their fluency partnerships for six minutes each day. Emphasize that the partnership is a working relationship and not necessarily a friendship. You may want to give an example of cooperation in a workplace, explaining that we may not like everyone we work with and may not want to be close friends with them, but we still treat co-workers with respect.
   - You may wish to share with the class that fluency partnerships were assigned by computer software if that model of selection was used. Generally speaking, if the concept of partnership is discussed completely with the class, there are few problems within the partnership. Occasionally, however, there may be two students who simply do not work well together. In that case, you may need to reassign partners.
5. Assign partners.
   - Announce the fluency partnerships and name one student as Partner 1 and the other student as Partner 2. (Partner 1 is the stronger reader, but do not share this information with students.) Simply state that Partner 1 always reads first for management purposes.
   - Let students know where they will sit during fluency practices. For example, some teachers make a seating arrangement for the language arts period that places partners next to each other. Other teachers have Partner 1 move beside Partner 2's desk.
   - This is an excellent time to set rules about the appropriate noise levels expected during fluency practice. Remind students that half of the class

will be reading aloud at the same time, and that the only people who need to hear them are their fluency partners.

Note: You may want to have students practice the procedures with partners other than those they will be actually assigned to. When students feel comfortable with the procedure, they can be placed with their assigned fluency partners.

6. Explain the procedure.
   - Inform the class as to where the *Practice Passages* and partnership portfolios will be stored.
   - Instruct students in the proper care and handling of the sponges and pens.
7. Have students practice together.
   - Detail the procedures for the students: Partner 1 always reads first, which means Partner 2 has the marking pen and marks errors and the stopping point.
   - Determine that the students are ready to start and set the timer for one minute. Announce, "Please begin." Monitor for any problems during the first timing.
   - When the timer sounds, say, "Stop." Instruct all the Partner 2s to make a diagonal mark after the last word read and to tell their partners which words were missed and the number of correct words read per minute. Remind Partner 2s to follow the appropriate error-correction procedure (as in *Figure 3.1*). Partner 1s then record the data on their *Fluency Graphs* or *Fluency Records*. Quickly check the work of various partners to ascertain that the initial timing data has been recorded correctly.
   - Announce when it is time for the second timing. In this timing, Partner 2 reads and Partner 1 uses the pen to track, record errors, and mark the stopping point. Remind students to follow the recording and error-correction procedures. Ask all the Partner 2s to fill in their *Fluency Graphs* or *Fluency Records*.

   Note: We recommend that students receive another complete training practice using the same *Practice Passages* and fluency partnerships the following day. This ensures that students understand the tracking, recording, and error-correction procedures and that they can perform them accurately.

Additional Tips

- After students are fully trained in the fluency practice procedures, on the first day of the week, give each student partnership a new *Practice Passage* to read. Students need a minimum of three to five rereadings each week of the same passage. Both student partners have the same passage, so both hear it read twice each day. Also, during the first actual fluency practice session, ask all students to first silently read their new *Practice Passages* to figure out if there are any unknown words. If a word is unknown by both partners, have students raise their hands to receive individual assistance.

  Note: The silent reading warm-up should only occur on the first day of a new *Practice Passage* each week.

- Remind students that they are responsible for keeping to the six-minute time frame:

1 minute for the partners to get ready.
1 minute for Partner 1 to read.
1 minute for Partner 2 to tell Partner 1 the total number of words read, the errors, corrections, and cwpm; and for Partner 1 to record the data. Then the procedure is reversed, with Partner 2 reading and Partner 1 noting the cwpm, etc.

See *Table I.1* in the *Introduction* for a more detailed outline of the six minutes.

- Teach students to return their partnership portfolios, with all the materials, to the designated location.
- Depending on students' reading abilities, but generally once a week, have students exchange their *Practice Passages* for new ones at the *same instructional reading level.* The reading level of the *Practice Passages* is only changed after teacher review and assessment. Do not allow students to remain on a *Practice Passage* so long that they memorize it.
- Schedule additional time (beyond the six minutes) on the first day of the week or on whatever day the *Practice Passages* will be exchanged for new ones. Students can easily be trained to exchange their own passages.
- The sponges may become sour if they are not washed weekly. Establish a routine to wash them on the same day that *Practice Passages* are exchanged. Usually a student can be assigned to handle this task.
- Continually monitor students closely during the fluency practices.

Generally speaking, fluency partners provide accountability for each other. Occasionally, a partnership may appear to be awarding inflated scores. A word or two in private to the "offenders" should solve the problem, along with maintaining close proximity while the "suspect" partnership is conducting their timings.

Student Progress and Record Keeping

Record keeping is an essential component of the *Six-Minute Solution*. It is critical to monitor improvement and make instructional decisions based on individual student progress. This may be accomplished by using either the *Fluency Graphs* or the *Fluency Records* (see *Appendix*). Teach students how to graph their own progress. Students tend to enjoy using the *Fluency Graphs* and *Fluency Records,* as they make it easy for them to see their progress. Graphs can be especially motivating to students who have not had much reading success in the past. It gives them a concrete way to see their reading skills improve.

As a general rule, students who are repeatedly reading passages at the correct instructional level make weekly progress—even if only by an increase of a few correct words per minute. Give special attention to any student whose reading rates are not increasing from week to week.

Determine whether students are reading at the expected rate for their instructional reading levels (see *Table 1.1* in *Chapter 1*). Remember, students should read at the rate commensurate with their instructional reading levels and not their grade-level placements. Reading rates increase as students are able to read more difficult material.

Check your students' *Fluency Records* or *Fluency Graphs* on a regular basis in order to determine that:

- Adequate progress is being made.
- Students have been assigned appropriate *Practice Passages*—neither too easy nor too hard.
- Students have been assigned appropriate fluency partners.
- It is the appropriate time to increase the difficulty level of the *Practice Passages* being used by partners.

Making Instructional Decisions Based on Fluency Graphs

The following examples demonstrate how the information on a student's *Fluency Record* or *Fluency Graph* can help you make important instructional decisions.

Example 1: Kevin

Kevin is a fifth-grade student with a second-grade instructional reading level. Based on *Table 1.1,* he is within the expected reading rate for his instructional level. Kevin is also making adequate progress. The first five days on his *Fluency Graph* (*Figure 4.1*) reflect rereading the same *Practice Passage.* His first reading on Monday was 60 cwpm. After practicing the passage four more times, his ending fluency rate was 70 cwpm.

Notice what happens the following week (March 9th). Kevin is now reading a new *Practice Passage.* However, his beginning fluency rate has increased by five words (60 to 65) when compared to the previous Monday—even though this is a brand new *Practice Passage.* As he continued to practice this passage during the second week, his reading rate has steadily improved. As Kevin's reading rate continues to improve and he begins to approach 80 correct words per minute, he will most likely be ready to start practicing third-grade *Practice Passages*. As a student reading third-grade material, his expected fluency rate goal would increase to 80–115 cwpm.

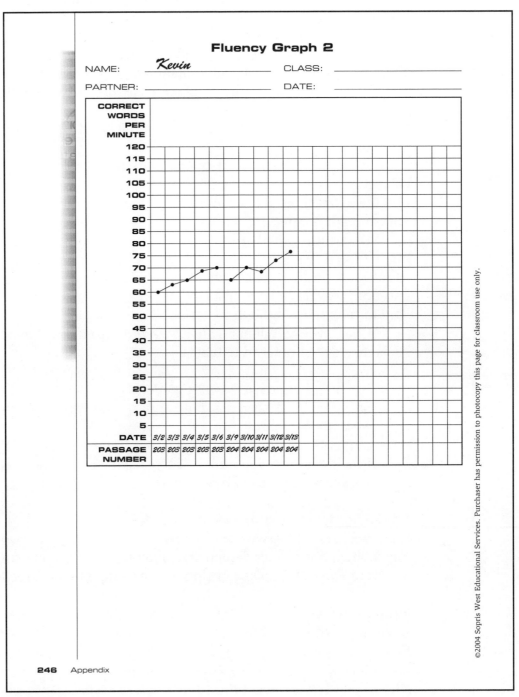

Figure 4.1
Kevin's *Fluency Graph*

Example 2: Sarita

Sarita is reading at a third-grade instructional reading level and was assigned a third-grade level *Practice Passage*. Based on *Table 1.1*, the appropriate goal for Sarita is to read between 80 and 115 cwpm.

A glance at Sarita's *Fluency Graph* (*Figure 4.2*) reveals that she is reading significantly below her expected range. In this case, the teacher decides that he needs to reevaluate whether or not Sarita has been placed correctly at her instructional level. Based on this reevaluation, the teacher will decide whether or not to lower the *Practice Passage* reading level assigned to Sarita, whether to add practice with the *Automatic Word Lists,* or whether to incorporate additional instructional strategies such as the ones in the following section, *Helping the Student Who Is Not Making Adequate Progress.* (See *Practice Passages & Automatic Word Lists* for how to choose and use the *Automatic Word Lists* with your students.)

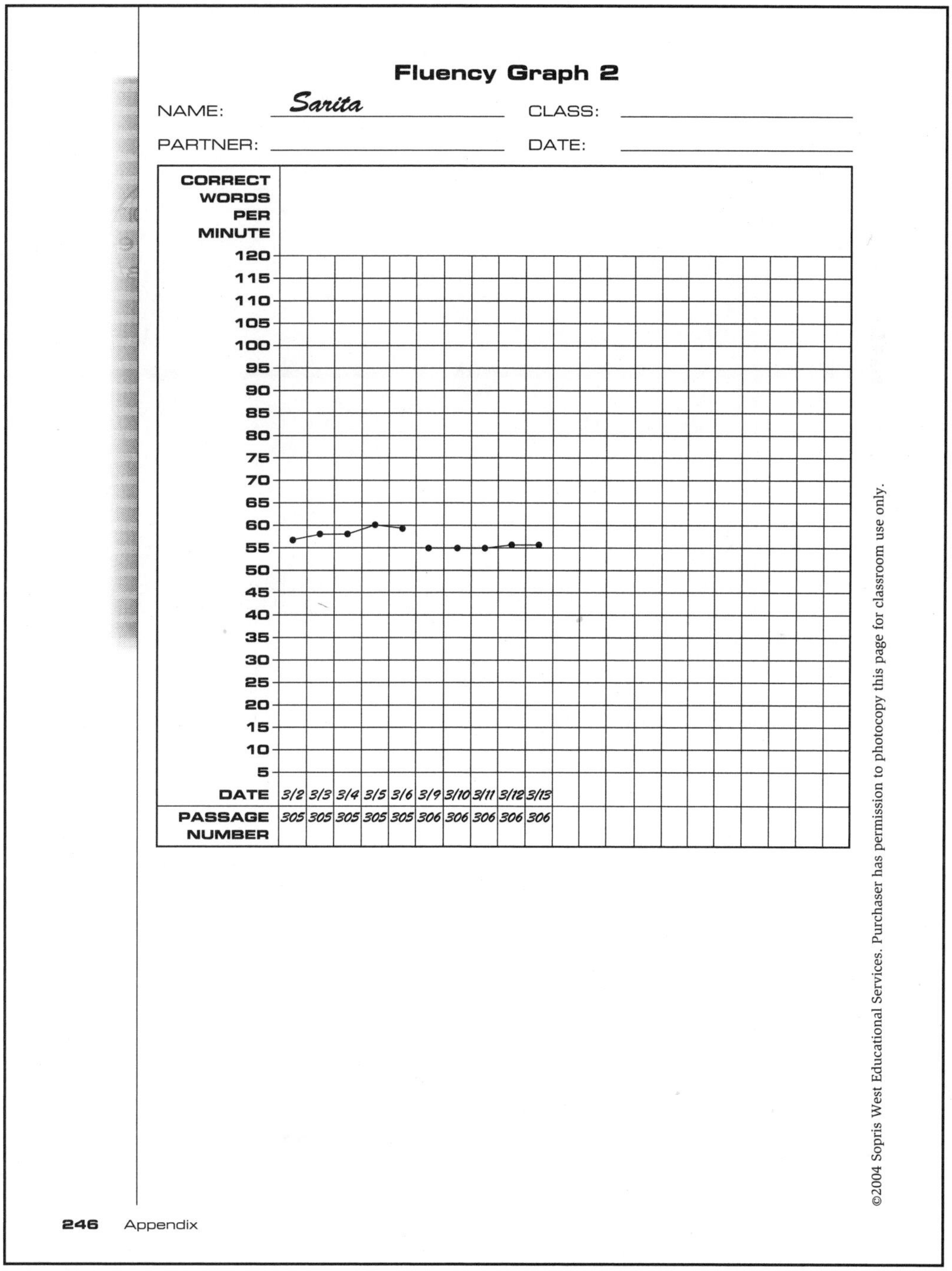

Figure 4.2
Sarita's *Fluency Graph*

Example 3: Jose

Jose is a seventh-grade student with a seventh-grade instructional reading level. His fluency goal, as shown on *Table 1.1*, is 180 cwpm. When Jose's teacher reviewed his *Fluency Graph* (*Figure 4.3*), she noticed that his reading rate is above his goal rate. She decided to assign eighth-grade-level *Practice Passages* to Jose, which may be more challenging for him.

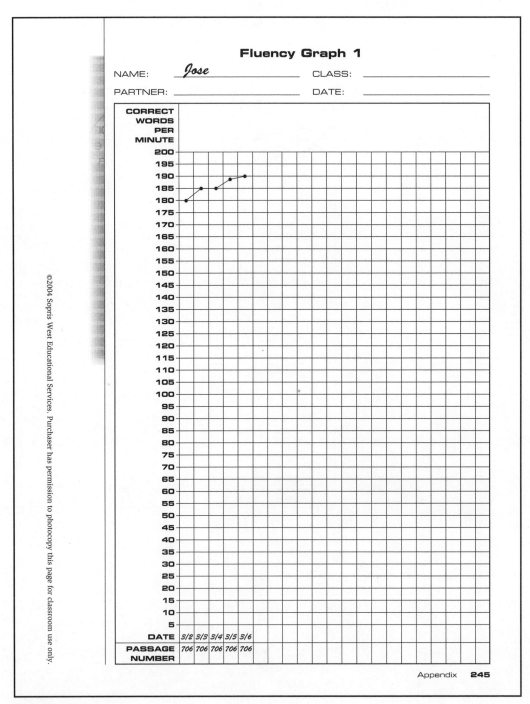

Figure 4.3
Jose's *Fluency Graph*

Helping the Student Who Is Not Making Adequate Progress

If a student is not making progress in the passage fluency and word-building activities contained in the *Six-Minute Solution*, it may be that the assigned *Practice Passages* do not match the instructional reading level. Students must be placed at the correct instructional reading levels in order to make the expected progress. When students practice fluency at their correct instructional levels, the vast majority make excellent progress. However, if after examining a student's *Fluency Graph* or *Fluency Record*, you determine that little progress has been made in two or more weeks, consider the following:

- If a student is in the third grade or higher, and reads less than 40 cwpm, an intensive comprehensive reading program should be used instead of or in addition to the *Six-Minute Solution*. A student who does not read above 40 cwpm needs explicit instruction in underlying reading skills before reading fluency can be developed.
- Read the *Practice Passage* with the student to ascertain if the student has been placed at the correct instructional reading level. The student should be able to read correctly approximately 95 percent of the words when reading at the appropriate instructional reading level. Note the errors the student is making. Perhaps many of the words the student is having difficulty with are high-frequency sight words. In this case, the student is likely to benefit from additional practice using the *Automatic Word Lists*. These lists contain sets of the most encountered, i.e., high-frequency, words in the written English language.
- If you observe that a student is having great difficulty reading an assigned *Practice Passage*, place the student in a *Practice Passage* that is one grade-level below the current passage. If the student reads less than 95 percent of the words correctly in the new passage, have the student read a *Practice Passage* at an even lower reading-level.
- A student's reading fluency problems may be associated with poor decoding skills. Assess whether the student would benefit from extra instruction in decoding.
- When students are first presented with new *Practice Passages*, make a point of meeting with the partnerships of struggling readers to ensure that they have adequate accuracy. Consistently and carefully monitor partnerships of struggling readers throughout the week.
- A stronger reader may be paired with a struggling reader as a "practice partner." This stronger reader reads the *Practice Passage* while the struggling reader follows closely behind, "echoing" the words of the stronger reader. The struggling reader gains additional reading strength by having the passage read almost simultaneously. The "practice partnership" session would occur in addition to the regular *Six-Minute Solution* sessions.
- Give fluency partners extra untimed reading-practice opportunities. Partners can whisper-read to each other, thus gaining additional rereadings of the same *Practice Passage* before taking their "formal" one-minute timings. Whisper-reading helps to build the confidence of struggling readers before their actual word counts are recorded.

- Fluency partners may also "ping-pong read" sentences back and forth to each other as another form of practice. This helps them to gain confidence and familiarity with the passage prior to the formal fluency timing.

Comprehension Strategies

Comprehension strategies (e.g., summarizing and paraphrasing) and the use of graphic organizers can be taught to students and practiced using the *Six-Minute Solution*. It is recommended that students be taught comprehension strategies and how to use graphic organizers directly through modeling and guided practice, bolstered by independent practice. Oral activities can easily be extended into a mini-lesson on how to take notes on expository material using the indentation note-taking strategy as described in the *Skills for School Success Series* (Archer and Gleason, 2002). Examples of effective comprehension strategies for nonfiction include:

- Summarizing
- Paraphrasing
- Retelling
- Describing
- Learning expository text structure.

Summarizing

One method of improving students' comprehension skills is to teach *summarizing*. First, model summarizing by pausing after reading aloud each paragraph of a *Practice Passage* from an overhead transparency.

Then "think aloud" while you determine the main idea of the paragraph. It is important to limit the number of words in the summary. Counting the words as they are spoken is a powerful way to illustrate this concept. Another effective way of teaching summarizing is to use the "paragraph shrinking" techniques from *PALS: Peer-Assisted Learning Strategies* (Fuchs, Fuchs, Kazlan, and Allen, 1999).

Once you have modeled summarizing, you can assign each partner an alternate paragraph to summarize from their *Practice Passages*. Then have the partners practice summarizing the whole passage. Encourage them to formulate a summary statement about the entire passage.

With additional instruction, this oral summarization practice can be extended to summary writing. After students complete their oral summarizations, ask them to turn over the *Practice Passage* and write a short summary.

Paraphrasing

To model *paraphrasing*, read aloud a *Practice Passage*, paragraph by paragraph, from an overhead transparency. After reading each paragraph, stop and announce, "I can put the information from this paragraph into my own words by saying. . . ."

Point out to students that it is easier to learn new information when you put it into your own words instead of trying to remember the text's language. Now have partners paraphrase alternate paragraphs of their *Practice Passages*. An effective method for teaching paraphrasing is to use the "read–cover–recite–check" strategy from the *Skills for School Success Series* (Archer and Gleason, 2002).

Retelling

Read aloud a *Practice Passage* from an overhead transparency. Then model a brief *retelling,* using the main ideas of the paragraphs to formulate the retelling. By using phrases such as "The passage began with," "Next I read," and "Then I learned," you can effectively model retelling of nonfiction text.

Describing

You can model *describing* by listing the characteristics, features, and examples of a topic. As you model, include key vocabulary words generally found in descriptive texts, such as "for example," "characteristics," "for instance," "such as," and "to illustrate." You may use a spider-web graphic organizer (as in *Figure 5.1*) in which the topic of the passage is listed in a circle in the center and the features are written on lines sticking out from the circle, forming a "web."

Students can then take turns orally describing their *Practice Passage* paragraphs for their partners and taking notes on the passage.

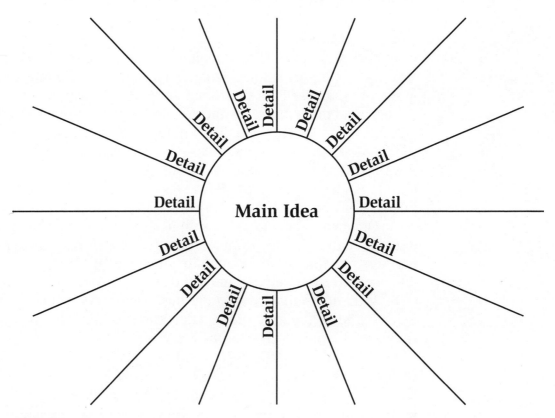

Figure 5.1
Spider-Web Graphic Organizer

Learning Expository Text Structure

Students can be taught about how text is structured using the following methods:

- Sequencing
- Comparing
- Analyzing cause and effect
- Problem-solving.

Sequencing

Some of the *Practice Passages* are sequential. They list items or events in numerical or chronological order. When teaching students a comprehension strategy for this type of passage, call attention to key vocabulary words, such as "first," "second," "third," "next," "then," "finally," "yesterday," "today," "now," "later," "before," and "after." Extend this sequencing comprehension activity to include writing by using a graphic organizer to list information sequentially (see *Figure 5.1*).

Comparing

Some of the *Practice Passages* explain how two or more things are alike or different. Call attention to key vocabulary in these passages, such as "alike," "same as," "different from," "in contrast," "on the other hand," "but," "yet," "however," "although," "opposite of," "as well as," "while," and "unless." Venn diagrams are excellent graphic organizers for showing the similarities and differences in comparison text. A Venn diagram consists of two or more overlapping circles (see *Figure 5.2*).

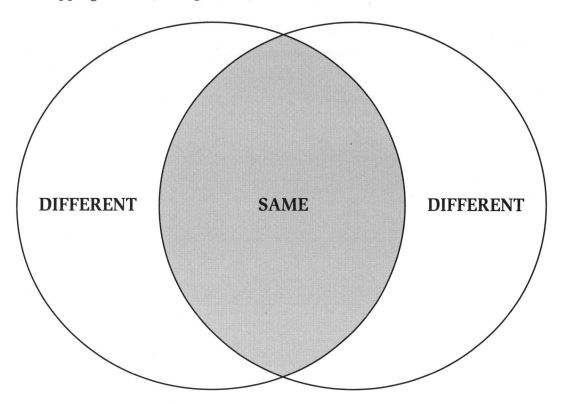

Figure 5.2
Venn Diagram

Analyzing Cause and Effect

Another type of expository text structure lists one or more causes and the resulting effect(s). Key vocabulary for this type of text includes "consequently," "because," "if . . . then," "thus," "since," "never the less," "accordingly," "because of," "as a result of," "may be due to," "therefore," and "this led to." A graphic organizer may be used to illustrate cause and effect (see *Figure 5.3*).

Chapter 5: Comprehension Strategies　**33**

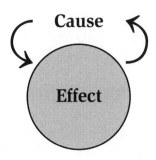

Figure 5.3
Cause and Effect Graphic Organizer

Problem-Solving

This type of expository text structure states a problem and lists one or more solutions. Key vocabulary includes "the problem is," "the question is," "furthermore," "one reason for," "a solution," and "another possibility." An example of a graphic organizer for problem–solution text is shown in *Figure 5.4*.

Problem:

Solutions:

Figure 5.4
Problem-Solving Graphic Organizer

More Than Six Minutes a Day

One of the advantages of the *Six-Minute Solution* fluency partner model is that students are able to increase their oral-reading fluency in only six minutes of an instructional period. The *Six-Minute Solution's* original grouping configuration is a partnership match based on instructional reading and fluency levels. By utilizing this configuration, the partnership is self-supporting. Each partner's reading level and cwpm mirror the other's. In this way, partnerships can function independently with little supervision. However, there might be times when you will need to devote more than six minutes a day to fluency practice, as in the following situations:

- On the first day of the week (when partnerships receive new *Practice Passages*), more time will be required. Each student in the partnership silently reads the entire new passage. If any words are unknown, students consult first with their partners. If neither partner knows a word, supply the correct pronunciation.
- Although the program can be easily implemented in a class of struggling readers, at times some students may require additional time in order to implement the *Six-Minute Solution* instructional strategies.
- Some grouping configurations, such as a small-group "literature circle" or a guided reading group, require more than six minutes a day.
- If you are incorporating additional comprehension activities, such as summary writing, additional time will be required.

Practice Passages

Materials that are well organized and easily accessible help to prevent the loss of valuable instructional time and reduce opportunities for off-task behavior. The following ideas will help you better manage the *Six-Minute Solution Practice Passages*:

In order to easily note the reading levels of the *Practice Passages* without making it obvious to students, the passages have been number-coded by grade level. For example, the first-grade passages start at 100 and the second-grade passages start at 200. You might also use color-coding to easily identify the reading levels (e.g., code all first-grade passages as yellow and all second-grade passages as green).

Use one portfolio (folder with two pockets) for each fluency partnership. The portfolio holds two copies of the grade-level *Practice Passage* currently being worked on. (Place each passage in a plastic sleeve or laminate.) It also holds two copies of the *Fluency Record* or *Fluency Graph* (see *Appendix),* and a small plastic bag with a water-based ink pen and a small, dampened sponge. Students mark their partners' errors with the marking pen on the laminated *Practice Passage,* then erase the marks before the next student reads. All of these materials can stay in the portfolio for the week and be easily changed each subsequent week.

After the three-to-five scheduled timings on the same *Practice Passages* have taken place for the week, replace them with new ones. Better yet, establish a routine in which student partners exchange old passages for new ones. Simply have them return completed passages to the file box and retrieve a new like-colored or like-numbered passage.

Establish a routine (preferably at least once a month) in which each student's *Fluency Graph* is checked. (This will ensure that each student has been placed at the correct instructional level and that all students are progressing towards their fluency goals.) If a student consistently reaches the upper limit of the range for the assigned grade-level *Practice Passages,* advance the student to the next grade-level of passages (see *Table 1.1*.) If one partner has met the goal while the other has not, then both students should be assigned new partners at their commensurate instructional reading levels. Likewise, if a partner does not seem to be making fluency gains, consider assigning the student to an easier reading level for a short period of time. It may be necessary to reassign partners so that students are working at their appropriate instructional reading levels. Switching two or more partnerships at the same time will serve to prevent embarrassment for students since no partnership is singled out. Most of the time, however, partners will progress at the same rate, since they were initially evenly matched.

At least once a week, soak the sponges in a liquid soap. A quick rinse in a white-vinegar-and-water solution and a good squeeze (to remove excess moisture) will prevent the sponges from souring. You may assign a student to this task.

Level 1 Practice Passages

101	All About Plants
102	Cat Families: It's All Relative
103	Rome Becomes an Empire
104	Flying Fish
105	Railroads in the West
106	Trees: Our Helpers
107	The Moon: Earth's Natural Satellite
108	Stars and Stripes: The First American Flag
109	Gifts from the Ancient Greeks
110	The Roaring '20s: The Age of Jazz
111	Hawaiian Islands
112	Oil: Black Gold
113	The Sun and Energy
114	Plants Are Alike and Different, Too!
115	Gold Rush in California
116	The Nile River in Ancient Egypt
117	Log Cabins: Pioneer Homes
118	Eli Whitney and the Cotton Gin
119	Earth: Hometown Planet
120	The Secret of Silk

All About Plants

There are many plants on our earth. Plants can be big. Plants can be small. We can't even see some plants. They are too small. Plants need many things to grow. They need sunlight. Other plants need a lot of sunlight. Others need very little sunlight. Plants also need water to grow. Just like sunlight, some plants need a lot of water. Other plants need very little water. A cactus can live without a lot of water.

Plants also need food from the soil to grow. Plants use their roots to get food and water from the soil. The roots also hold up the plant. The leaves make food for the plant. They use the sun to make food. Stems are different on plants. The stem holds up the leaves and flowers on the plant. It also carries water and food to the plant. The stem of a tree is hard and strong. The stem of a flower can bend easily. Plants have seeds to grow new plants. Some seeds are very small. Other seeds are in fruit that grow on the plants. Some plants have flowers. Other plants do not have flowers. Plants give us many things. They are good to us.

Total Words Read _____
− Errors _____
= CWPM _____

Cat Families: It's All Relative

Did you know that all cats are related? Small house cats and wild lions belong to the same family. They have a lot of things in common. For example, all cats have long claws. They use these claws to grip and tear. Cats keep their claws sharp by scraping them on rough things like tree trunks. Pet owners give house cats scratching posts to use. All cats walk on their toes. Their heels do not touch the ground. Cats have five toes on each front foot. But their back feet only have four toes. Small pads on cats' feet help them to move quietly. Most cats hunt at night. They have a good sense of smell, sharp hearing, and can see well at night. Cats are graceful animals. They are able to climb and balance themselves very well. Cats are able to run quickly and make great leaps.

Cats that live in homes are called house cats. Cats are not as friendly as dogs. But they are neat and need less care than dogs. There are two kinds of house cats. One kind has long hair and the other has short hair. Pet cats should be given a warm, dry box for sleeping. They need two or three meals each day.

House cats make very good pets for some people.

Rome Becomes an Empire

The Romans wanted a big empire. The army was very big. Soldiers signed up for twenty years. Each soldier did the job well. Some were archers. There were spear throwers. Others were horse riders. The army had many parts. Each part was called a legion. A legion had six thousand men. There were nurses, cooks, and arrow makers. Often there were long battles. They did not need to return to Rome for supplies.

The Romans built roads. This helped them to control the empire. There were more than fifty thousand miles of roads. The roads were built to last. The roads had three layers. First, the men dug the road. The bed of the road was filled with rocks. They mixed gravel and concrete. This was put on the rocks. Flat paving stones were on top. Stone curbs were on each side. They dug drainage ditches. There was a ditch on each side of the road. Many people used the roads. Farmers used the roads for trade. The army used the roads to get places fast.

The Romans wanted to keep the empire. The empire spread to many places. It was very big.

Flying Fish

Did you know that some fish can fly? It is true! They do not really fly like birds. But some fish can glide through the air. These fish are called flying fish. They have long fins on either side of their bodies. When a flying fish leaves the water, it spreads its fins. The air catches under the fins. The air under the fins helps the fish glide. Flying fish can glide at speeds of 40 miles per hour. They can go as far as 30 meters before they splash down.

The flying fish also has a special tail. Its tail is in two parts. Each part of its tail can move very fast. Those two tail parts help the flying fish to swim very fast. The tail also helps to propel the fish out of the water. You may ask yourself, "Why would a fish want to fly?" The reason is that the flying fish is trying to get away from a bigger fish. When a flying fish is being chased, it swims fast to the top of the water. Then it leaps out of the water. As it leaps, the flying fish spreads its fins and glides away from danger.

Total Words Read _____
- Errors _____
= CWPM _____

Railroads in the West

Before railroads, it took a long time to go from New York to San Diego. Most people used a horse and wagon to cross the U.S. Some people sailed around Cape Horn. Either way, it took three months. People wanted to travel faster.

The U.S. had no money to build the train tracks. So the U.S. gave two groups land. Right-of-way land was for the train tracks. The U.S. also gave large pieces of land for every mile of track that was laid. This land could be sold. The groups sold some of the land. The groups used the money to buy materials. Workers had to be paid.

The Union Pacific group started in Nebraska. They laid the tracks toward the west. The Central Pacific group began on the West Coast. They laid the tracks to the east.

Both groups worked hard. They had to cross rivers. Bridges were built. There were tall mountains. The men had to dig tunnels. It was not easy work. The tracks met in Utah. The last spike was made of gold. A silver hammer was used. The track was finished.

Now people could cross the U.S. in one week. More people moved to the West.

Total Words Read _____

− Errors _____

= CWPM _____

Trees: Our Helpers

Trees help all of us. Trees give us wood. We use the wood to build our houses. We have doors on our houses made from wood. The chairs we sit on are made from wood. Our houses have many things made from wood. Trees keep us dry if it is raining. Trees also keep us cool in the shade with their leaves.

Paper is made from trees. Many other things come from trees. Fruits such as apples and oranges grow on trees. Cherries and peaches come from trees, too. Walnuts and almonds grow on trees. Maple syrup for pancakes comes from maple trees. Birds live in trees. Many animals also live in trees.

Trees help us when we are sick. Many medicines are made from trees. When trees die, they still help us. They help to make new soil for seeds to grow. They also become homes for animals such as rabbits. Bees put their hives in fallen trees. Trees help the earth, too. The tree's leaves work with the sun to make oxygen. Without oxygen, we could not live. Trees are very important to us. Trees help us all in many, many ways. We should take care of our trees because they take care of us.

Total Words Read _____
− Errors _____
= CWPM _____

The Moon: Earth's Natural Satellite

On a clear night, the moon can be seen. The moon is a bright object in the sky. Only the sun is brighter. The moon is thousands of miles away. The moon is much smaller than the earth. The moon travels around the earth. It takes about 27 days to make one orbit. Each night it is in a different place in its trip around the earth. More or less light from the sun gets to the moon. The moon reflects sunlight. Each night the moon looks different. Sometimes it looks like a big ball. Other nights it looks like a thin light. Sometimes there is no moon at all. It is a full moon when the entire surface of the moon reflects sunlight.

The moon is not like the earth. No one lives on the moon. It is very rocky. There are no plants or animals. During the day it is very hot. Sometimes it is two hundred degrees. At night, it is very cold. It can be 250 degrees below zero.

Men have visited the moon. They had to wear space suits. They did not stay long. They put up a U.S. flag. Moon rocks were brought back to Earth. There is not much on the moon. People have always enjoyed looking at the moon at night. They probably always will.

Stars and Stripes: The First American Flag

0	It is said that Betsy Ross made the first U.S. flag. It was called the Stars
16	and Stripes. It had thirteen rows of stripes. The top row was red. The next
31	row was white. The next row was red and so on. In the top left was a field
49	of blue. There were thirteen stars. Each star had five points. One point was
63	upward. They were arranged in a circle. At that time, there were thirteen
76	colonies. Each star was for a colony. The first flag was raised on July 1, 1776.
92	When the U.S. became a nation, the stars stood for each state. As the
106	U.S. grew, a star was added for each state. At first, a stripe was also added.
122	One time the flag had fifteen stripes and fifteen stars. Then the U.S. decided
136	to keep the thirteen stripes. The stripes were for the thirteen colonies. When
149	a state joined the U.S., a new star was added. The order of the stars was
165	changed many times. Hawaii became a state in 1959. The last star was
178	added for Hawaii.
181	Now there are fifty stars on the flag. The flag still has thirteen stripes.
195	If another state joined the U.S., a star would be added.
206	

Total Words Read _____

− Errors _____

= CWPM _____

Gifts from the Ancient Greeks

The ancient Greeks lived close to the sea. Many lived on islands. The farmers grew crops all year. The winters were mild. It was sunny in the summer. They grew grapes, olives, wheat, and barley. The Greeks had many ships. They traded with others. To make it easy, they used coins. The coins were made of gold and silver.

The Greeks had city-states. There was no king. The power was in the hands of the citizens. There were rich and poor people. The men citizens voted. They made the rules. When someone broke a rule, they had a trial. The people served on juries. Most people lived in the city. Some farmed land around the city. Sometimes they had wars. The wars were over land. Some people moved. They made new city-states.

The Greeks liked to have fun. They also wanted to honor their gods. Every four years they had sports events. There were foot races and wrestling. They threw discs. The sports events were called the Olympics. Two times each year they went to plays. The dramas were very good. The plays told stories about gods and history. Most of the plays were very sad. A few were very funny. They were always sad at the end. A jury voted for the best play.

The Greeks had many good ideas. Many movies are based on their stories. The name and dates are changed. People like to go to sports events. Coins are used to buy and sell things. Citizens vote and make rules.

Practice Passage 110

The Roaring '20s: The Age of Jazz

0	After World War I, the U.S. was ready for change. People started to
13	change in the way they did things. They wanted to find new ways to express
28	themselves. Music was one way to enjoy life. The music that most people in
42	the U.S. liked was jazz. They saw jazz as a way to break away from old
58	rules. It was a way to be free.
66	Black people in the U.S. created jazz. It started in New Orleans. It
79	grew out of music called the blues. The blues was based on the hard life of
95	most blacks. The music told sad stories. It helped people cope with hard
108	times. Most of the black people who played jazz had no formal schooling in
122	music. Yet, they were great performers.
128	There was no right way to play jazz. It was about how people felt. It
143	was based on a theme or musical idea. The players chased a tune up and
158	down the scales as they played. This gave the player a sense of being free.
173	At the same time, young women wanted to be free of old ideas. They
187	cast out long, full dresses. They put on short skirts. They had loose-fitting
201	clothes. The young women cut their hair short. Women wore makeup. They
213	danced to jazz music. These women were called "flappers."
222	Today women wear clothes they like. They cut their hair many ways.
234	People still like to listen to jazz.
241	

Total Words Read _____

− Errors _____

= CWPM _____

Hawaiian Islands

0	Captain Cook was the first white man to visit Hawaii. He landed in the
14	islands in 1778. The islands were very pretty. There was sun every day.
27	Palm trees grew there. There were flowers all year. Ships going to and from
41	Asia stopped in the islands. Sometimes sailors jumped ship. They did not
53	want to leave.
56	A king ruled Hawaii. Farmers from the U.S. moved to the islands. They
69	grew pineapples and sugar. The king let the U.S. build a navy base. The
83	king died. His sister became the queen. She was removed from the throne.
96	The islands became part of the U.S. The navy base grew larger. More people
110	moved to the islands. Hawaii became a state in 1959.
120	Many people like to visit the islands. They come by plane and ship.
133	The sun shines all year. There are lots of palm trees and flowers. Birds live
148	in the trees. The birds sing all of the time. People like to play in the sun.
165	They swim in the sea. A few like to surf. Many people play golf. Some like
181	to hike in the hills. Most like to listen to the music and watch the dances.
197	The islands are fun to visit.
203	

Total Words Read _____

− Errors _____

= CWPM _____

Oil: Black Gold

0	Oil is sometimes called "black gold." Oil is used for many things. It is
14	worth a lot of money. Oil made some people very rich. At one time oil was
30	not worth much. People did not like oil on their land. It was dirty. Oil smelled
46	bad. Plants did not grow well near oil. That was two hundred years ago.
60	The first oil well was in Pennsylvania. People used oil as a medicine.
73	This did not work well. Oil was also used to grease metal parts. This made
88	machines run smoother. When oil is heated, dirt and grime go to the
101	bottom. The oil at the top is called refined oil. People found uses for refined
116	oil. It was used for lamps and stoves. Oil was sold in the grocery stores and
132	door-to-door. People did not need to make candles or buy whale oil.
146	Gasoline is high-grade refined oil. About one hundred years ago, people
158	started to use gas for cars. Oil was found in the West. People started to
173	search for oil. They drilled wells. At first oil was shipped east in barrels.
187	Then they used railroad tank cars. Finally, pipelines were laid. Oil is also
200	shipped in big oil tankers.
205	Today there are many uses for oil. It is used to heat houses, for fuel,
220	and as a cleaner. Now people would like to find oil on their land. They
235	would be very rich.
239	

Total Words Read _____

− Errors _____

= CWPM _____

Practice Passage 113

The Sun and Energy

0	The sun is a star. It is a star like the thousands of stars seen at night.
17	The sun is the closest star to earth. It is 93 million miles away. The sun is at
35	the center of the solar system. It is much bigger than the earth. It is made of
52	gas. The gas is on fire. In the center, there are many explosions. The sun is
68	hotter than hot. The heat causes a lot of light. It takes about eight minutes
83	for light to go from the sun to the earth. Animals and plants need the energy
99	that comes from the sunlight.
104	Light from the sun gives us energy. Plants need sunlight to grow. Trees
117	grow tall. People cut down trees for the wood. When wood is burned,
130	energy is released. Bugs and animals eat the plants. People eat plants and
143	animals to give them energy. Some plants and animals die. They stay in the
157	ground for millions of years. After a while, they turn into oil. Oil is used to
173	run cars and trucks. The heat from the sun warms the air near the ground.
188	The air gets warm and rises. This causes wind. Wind is a form of energy.
203	The sunlight gives us many forms of energy.
211	

Total Words Read _____

− Errors _____

= CWPM _____

Plants Are Alike and Different, Too!

There are so many plants on our earth. When we look at them, they all seem so different from one another. Yet, all of these very different plants are alike in some ways.

All plants need air, water, light, and minerals. Plants are alike in other ways, too. All plants have some sort of roots. Some roots may be close to the soil's surface. Some roots may go deeply down into the earth. Some roots may even grow on top of the soil. But all plants have roots.

All plants have stems. The stems may look different from one another. They may be short and narrow. They may be tall and thick. There may be many stems on a plant, or very few stems. The stems on trees are hard. The stems on roses have sharp thorns and are narrow. The stems on daisies are short and bend easily. The stems are a part of all plants. They may be different, but all plants have stems.

All plants have leaves. The leaves, just like the stems and roots, are different from one another. Some leaves are large, like those on palm trees. Some leaves are small and narrow. The spines on a cactus are its leaves. The pine needles on a pine tree are its leaves. Just like roots and stems, all plants have leaves, but they are very different from one another.

Gold Rush in California

0	In 1848, gold was found in California. It was found in a river. People
14	wanted to be rich. They wanted to find gold. Most of the people lived in the
30	East. People wanted to move west. They wanted to be the first to get gold.
45	There was a rush to find gold. Some people put everything in wagons.
58	Horses and oxen pulled the wagons. It was hard to travel in wagons. It was
73	a long trip. They had to cross rivers. The deserts had no water. The
87	mountains were tall. It took three months to get to the gold fields. Some
101	people came by ship. The ships sailed around Cape Horn. Everyone wanted
113	to get rich.
116	By 1850, many people lived in the West. People looked for gold in the
130	rivers. Some people dug mines. Mines were in the mountains and in the
143	deserts. A few people found gold. Some people opened stores. They sold
155	things to the miners. Some storeowners became very rich. Some people
166	farmed. They sold their goods to the miners. Soon there was not much gold
180	left. People found other jobs. Most people liked the West. They liked the
193	sunshine. They did not move back East.
200	

Total Words Read _____

− Errors _____

= CWPM _____

Practice Passage 116

The Nile River in Ancient Egypt

0	The Nile River is in Egypt. It is the longest river in the world. The Nile
16	is four thousand miles long. The river flows north. Egypt gets almost no
29	rain. On both sides of the river, there is a desert. There are tall mountains in
45	Central Africa. This is where the river begins. Each year it rains and the
59	snow melts. The level of the Nile rises.
67	A long time ago, there were no dams on the Nile. Each year, the level
82	of the Nile rose. The water flowed over the banks of the river. There were
97	big floods. Black river mud covered the land. The mud was good for
110	growing crops. Farmers used the water for crops. They dug ditches to move
123	the water. Little dams were built in the ditches. Farmer saved the water for
137	the crops.
139	The river had many other uses. Boats sailed on the Nile. Animals lived
152	along the river. There were ducks, little birds, and fish. One river plant was
166	useful. Papyrus is reed. It is a tall, thin plant. The plant grows wild by the
182	river. It was used for boats, baskets, and shoes. The plant was cut into thin
197	layers. This made a kind of paper. The Nile River was very useful.
210	

Total Words Read _____

− Errors _____

= CWPM _____

Level 1 Practice Passages

Log Cabins: Pioneer Homes

In the U.S., log cabins were home for many people. During the 1700s and the 1800s, many people lived in log cabins. Most of the log cabins were on farms or in the woods. People built log cabins because there were lots of trees.

A log cabin was simple to make. An ax was needed to make a log cabin. The trees were cut down. The logs were notched. Then logs were joined at the corners. The logs are put together to make a square room. Log cabins were not big. They had one room. A chimney was at one end of the room. The chimney was made of rocks. The rocks were piled up high. Mud was put in the holes between the rocks. A family could make a log cabin in a few days.

Log cabins were not big. They were only as long and wide as tall trees. Some people made the log cabin bigger. They put boards in the rafters. This made a loft. They used ladders to get to the loft. Children slept in the loft. Some people built another log cabin room. Many people liked to live in log cabins.

Total Words Read _____

− Errors _____

= CWPM _____

Eli Whitney and the Cotton Gin

Cotton is an important crop. It grows on a plant in pods. Fluffy white fiber and black seeds are in the pod. It used to be hard to get the seeds off the fiber. In 1793, Eli Whitney made the cotton gin. The gin makes it easy to get the seeds off the fiber.

The cotton gin looks like a box. It is open at the top. There are little slits down one side. Cotton fiber and seeds are placed in the box. There is a roller outside the box. The roller is on one side of the box. Wire teeth are around the roller. People can turn the roller. When the roller is turned the teeth go into the box through the slits. The fiber in the box is caught in the wire teeth. As the teeth come out of the box, they pull fibers out. The seeds are wider than the slits. The seeds stay in the box. Another roller turns the other way. It takes the fibers from the first roller. The first roller turns back into the box. The first roller gets more fiber. Now it is easy to get the seeds off the fiber.

The cotton fiber is made into thread. The thread is used to make cloth. People like cotton clothes. Cotton clothes are cool in the summer. They are easy to wash. There is a demand for lots of cotton. Many farmers grow cotton.

Practice Passage 119

Earth: Hometown Planet

    0   The earth is one of the nine planets. It is the third planet from the sun.
  16   It is also the fifth largest planet. As far as we know, Earth is the only planet
  33   where there is life. There are many reasons for this. Earth is made up of
  48   land and water. There is more water than land on Earth. More than half of
  63   Earth is water. Humans need water to live. Earth is the only planet where
  77   water is in liquid form. That is why there are oceans on Earth. Oceans help
  92   keep the temperature stable. The greenhouse effect helps to warm the earth.
104   The earth is not too hot or cold for life. The earth's air has oxygen. The
120   earth's air also has carbon dioxide. Both are important for life.
131   The earth is four to five billion years old. But the surface of the earth is
147   very young. That means that it has changed often since it was formed. The
161   earth is a very big planet. It is also the densest of all the planets. The earth
178   turns around in a circle. It turns once a day. The earth goes around the sun.
194   When the earth turns to the sun, it is day. When it turns away from the sun,
211   it is night.
214

Total Words Read _____

− Errors _____

= CWPM _____

The Secret of Silk

Silk is strong, beautiful cloth. Silk was first made in China. No one else knew how to make silk. China guarded the secret. For thousands of years people had to buy silk from China. China would not let people come see how silk was made. China traded silk for gold, glass, and goods from the West.

It takes lot of work to make silk. Silkworms are fed mulberry leaves. After five weeks, each worm makes a cocoon. Workers gather the cocoons. They boil water in big pots. The cocoons are put in the hot water. This kills the worms. The hot water softens the cocoons. Workers carefully unwind silk threads. The thread is very long. Each thread is very thin. It can break easily. Thread from many cocoons is twisted together. This makes one strong silk thread. This thread can be twisted with other threads to make it stronger. The thread is washed. Silk is white. Most silk is dyed. There are many different colors of silk thread. The thread is made into cloth.

The silk is used to make many things. Most silk is used to make clothes. Sometimes silk thread is used to make rugs. The rugs are made of knotted silk threads. People like silk because it is beautiful and it lasts a long time.

Total Words Read _____
- Errors _____
= CWPM _____

Level 2 Practice Passages

201	The Panama Canal: A Sea Path
202	Mars: The Red Planet
203	Maps: How to Read Them
204	Baseball: A National Sport
205	Henry Ford: Automobile Manufacturer
206	The Model T: The Car That Changed America!
207	Garter Snakes
208	The Ancient Kingdom of Kush
209	Thomas Edison: An American Inventor
210	The Food Chain: A Cycle of Life
211	Rivers and Canals: Our Water Highways
212	Marco Polo: A World Traveler
213	The Great Wall: One of the World's Seven Wonders
214	The Louisiana Purchase: A Good Deal
215	Ben Franklin: Inventor and Statesman
216	Weather: It's What's Outside That Counts
217	Guide Dogs: Helpful Pets
218	Sharks: Amazing Fish
219	Roads and Highways
220	Chinese Kite Flying: A National Pastime

Practice Passage 201

The Panama Canal: A Sea Path

0	North and South America are joined by a little piece of land. Before
13	1900, it was hard to get from the East to the West Coast. Ships had to sail
30	around Cape Horn. It took three months to go from New York to San Diego.
45	People wanted a shorter trip.
50	The French started to dig a canal. It was hard work. Many workers
63	died of yellow fever. The French gave up. Doctors found a cure for yellow
77	fever. The U.S. made a deal to use the land in Panama. Men started to dig
93	the canal.
95	It took nine years to make the canal. It is 51 miles long. It goes
110	through two lakes. Workers cut a nine-mile path in the rock. The canal is
125	300 feet wide. The average depth is 120 feet. The canal was ready for use in
141	1914. It took a third of the time to sail from the West to the East.
157	Parts of the canal are above sea level. At one place, it is 85 feet above
173	the sea. How can this be? The canal uses locks to move ships. A lock is a
190	water-filled space. The space is like a big room. There is no roof. The room
206	is made of cement. There is a door on each end of the lock. One door of the
224	lock opens. The water level is raised. A ship moves into a lock. The other
239	door opens. The ship moves out of the lock. The ship sails into another lock.
254	The water level is raised again. The ship is 85 feet above sea level. The ship
270	sails into the canal. The ship sails into another lock. Water is let out of the
286	lock. The ship is now lower. The canal has three sets of locks.
299	Today many ships use the canal. The canal is very busy. Ships carry
312	many goods from one coast to the other. People take cruise ships through
325	the canal.
327	

Total Words Read _____

− Errors _____

= CWPM _____

Mars: The Red Planet

Mars is one of the nine planets. It is the fourth planet from the sun. Mars is the seventh largest planet. The planet Mars has a reddish color. So people call it the Red Planet. It was named because of its color. The month of March was named after the planet Mars. Mars was the name of the god of war. The ancient Greeks worshiped Mars. He was also called Ares.

Mars is the closest planet to Earth. When Mars is in the night sky, it can be very bright. Then people can see Mars. They do not even need a telescope.

Many spaceships have visited Mars. The first one to visit was in 1965. The last one was in 1997. The spaceships bring back clues about Mars. People study the clues. They learn about Mars this way.

Mars is a small planet. It is also rocky. Mars is a very cold planet. There is no water on Mars now. But there may have been water at one time. There are clues that lakes or oceans may have been on Mars. People think that there was water a very long time ago. They also think that the water was there for a short time. Some people think that there was life on Mars at one time. No one knows for sure. They must keep studying to find out.

Total Words Read _____
− Errors _____
= CWPM _____

Maps: How to Read Them

A map is an important tool. It is not hard to learn to read a map. There are four main directions on a map. They are north, east, south, and west. The sun rises in the east. It sets in the west. It is easy to find north and south. Point your right hand to the east. Point your left hand to the west. You will be looking at the north. South will be at the back of your head. On a map, the top is always north. The bottom is always south. The right side is east and the left is west. To help people remember the directions, there is usually a compass on the map with "N," "E," "S," and "W" at each of the four points. Each letter stands for one of the directions.

On a world map, the land is usually brown, yellow, and green. The brown areas stand for mountains. The yellow areas show the deserts. Green is used to show low areas where many plants grow. The water areas are blue. Across the middle is a line. This is the equator. This is not a real line. It is put on the world map to show the middle of the earth, where it is hot. In the north and south it is very cold. These areas are usually white. Sometimes there are red dots on a world map. These usually represent large cities. If there is a very big red dot, the city is very big. If there is a smaller red dot, the city is smaller.

If you know a few simple facts, maps are easy to read. Maps are very useful. People use them to find places and to get information.

Total Words Read _____
− Errors _____
= CWPM _____

Practice Passage 204

Baseball: A National Sport

0	Many people like to play baseball. The game started in 1839 in New
13	York. A teacher, Mr. Doubleday, laid out the field. He made up the rules. At
28	first, players did not wear gloves. They caught the ball with their bare
41	hands. This hurt their hands. In 1875, players started to wear gloves. In the
55	beginning, catchers did not wear masks. Balls would hit them in the face.
68	One catcher made a wire mask. Soon all of the catchers had masks. Now all
83	players wear gloves. Catchers wear masks. They also wear knee and chest
95	pads.
96	Most towns had teams. Many boys and men joined the teams. Some
108	teams were very good. People liked to watch teams play the game. They
121	wanted their team to win. Some teams started to pay players. People started
134	to pay money to watch the game. This was in 1868. Soon there were two
149	major baseball leagues. The first World Series was in 1903.
159	Now baseball is played everywhere. Little boys and girls play on town
171	teams. Baseball is played in schools. Adults play the game for fun. People
184	still like to watch baseball. They pay to watch the pros play. There are still
199	two major leagues. Most big cities have a major league team. Baseball is a
213	national sport.
215	

Total Words Read _____

− Errors _____

= CWPM _____

Henry Ford: Automobile Manufacturer

0	Many people think Henry Ford made the first auto. He did not. There
13	were autos since the 1890s. Each auto was made by hand. Only rich people
27	could own one. Mr. Ford had a dream. He wanted to make a car for all the
44	people. Mr. Ford wanted every family to own a car. He wanted to make cars
59	cheaply. Then a family could afford a car.
67	Mr. Ford made the Model T. It sold for $850. By 1916, he sold the
82	same car for $360. How did he do this? Mr. Ford used mass production. He
97	made many cars. They were all the same. Many workers put the cars
110	together. Each worker did one thing. One worker put on a top. Two workers
124	put on doors. Another put in a seat. The same model was made each year.
139	Year after year, it was the same car. The same car was made for ten years.
155	Everyone knew how to do the job well. There was a joke of the day: You
171	could have a Model T in any color you wanted as long as it was black.
187	The profit on each car was small. Every family wanted a car. Mr. Ford
201	sold lots of cars. He became very rich. Henry Ford's dream came true.
214	Today many families can have a car. Some families have more than one car.
228	

Total Words Read _____

− Errors _____

= CWPM _____

The Model T: The Car That Changed America!

0	For thousands of years, it was hard for people to travel. Then came the
14	Model T car. The Model T was cheap. Nearly every family could own the
28	car. A new car cost $360. A used car could be $25 to $50. Cars freed people.
45	Cars let them travel more than ever before. They could live out of town.
59	Men and women could drive to work. Families visited places far from home.
72	Cars had good and bad effects. Family trips were fun. People liked to
85	go sight-seeing. Often lots of people were in one car. Some people were
99	"back-seat drivers." Some were good drivers. Some were road hogs. A few
112	were bad drivers. By 1930 cars caused more than half of the accidental
125	deaths in the U.S.
129	Cars were good for business. Many people made cars. This was good
141	work. Steel was needed to make cars. More rubber was needed for tires. Cars
155	needed oil and gas to run. Gas stations opened all over the U.S. Some people
170	were needed to fix cars. Motels opened for people with cars. Places for
183	tourists to visit opened. More roads were built. Trucks carried goods from
195	place to place. It was easy for people to travel. Cars changed the way of life.
211	

Total Words Read _____

− Errors _____

= CWPM _____

Garter Snakes

0	Garter snakes make great pets. They live in many places. Garter snakes
12	live in gardens. They live near houses. They are often the first snake a child
27	sees. Children like to catch garter snakes. It is lucky that garters are safe
41	snakes. If someone comes near them, garters will hide. If someone tries to
54	fight, the garter will fight back. But garters never start a fight. They will never
69	attack people or pets first. Garter snakes live between three and ten years.
82	Some people call garter snakes "garden snakes." Other people call
92	them grass snakes. Garter snakes are usually striped. Some garter snakes
103	have red or yellow stripes. Their background color is plain or checked.
115	Garter snakes are not very big. Full-grown garter snakes are two to three
129	feet in length. They are also very narrow in width. Because they are small,
143	garters are quick to heat up. They are also quick to cool down. Garter
157	snakes sleep in the ground during the winter. They come out of the ground
171	in the spring. Garter snakes like to bask in the sun during the day.
185	Garter snakes eat insects. They also eat worms and frogs. Since they
197	are small, they are agile. This makes it easier for them to catch their prey.
212	Garters use their sight mostly to hunt their prey, although they can also "hear"
226	vibrations in the ground. Garters hunt during the cooler part of the day.
239	

Total Words Read _____

− Errors _____

= CWPM _____

The Ancient Kingdom of Kush

0	Kush was once part of Egypt. It was on the southern part of the Nile
15	River. Egypt became weak. The army was not strong. Priests and nobles
27	fought with the kings. Kush rulers broke away from Egypt. This was in 671
41	B.C. Kush built a capital in Meroe.
48	Meroe was a good place for a city. It had iron ore and lots of wood.
64	Workers knew how to make pure metal from ore. Brick ovens were used to
78	heat the iron ore. Bellows were used to make wood fires very hot. Pure iron
93	was used to make tools and weapons. Iron spears and swords were very
106	strong. They were stronger than bronze weapons. There were also many
117	artists in Meroe. They made beautiful bowls, vases, and jewelry. Meroe
128	became a trade center. Traders came from all around. They wanted iron and
141	artworks. They traded fine cloth, glass, skins, gold, silver, and ivory. Meroe
153	was a great city.
157	In A.D. 350, a nearby army came to Meroe. They made war. The people
171	did not fight back. Some people were killed. Many became slaves. A few ran
185	away. The army took food and iron. The army set fire to reed houses and
200	brick buildings. The whole city burned down. No one came back to the city.
214	That was the end of Kush.
220	

Total Words Read _____

− Errors _____

= CWPM _____

Thomas Edison: An American Inventor

0	Thomas A. Edison is a well-known inventor in the U.S. His most
13	famous invention was the electric light bulb. He put thin wire inside an
26	airless glass globe. It was not like the lights used today. It did not have a
42	steady light. The light bulb flickered. But it worked for forty hours. Soon the
56	light bulb worked longer. People started to use light bulbs in the house.
69	They did not need to use lamp oil or candles. The bulbs were safer. They
84	did not need to use fire for light.
92	Edison had many good ideas. People liked the "talking machine." This
103	was the first record player. The first "record" was made from a thin piece of
118	tin. The tin covered a tube. The tube slipped over a pipe-like part. Records
133	were hollow tubes. The tubes were covered with wax. It was years before
146	records were flat and round.
151	He had other good ideas. At first, films did not have sound. The words
165	were printed at the bottom of the film. People read the words and watched
179	the actors at the same time. Edison made records to go with the films.
193	People could hear what the actors had to say. Today people use things that
207	Thomas A. Edison invented.
211	

Total Words Read _____

− Errors _____

= CWPM _____

The Food Chain: A Cycle of Life

0	The food chain is a cycle. Plants need sunlight, air, and water to grow.
14	Plants grow almost everywhere on earth. Animals eat living things. Some
25	eat plants. Some eat other animals. Many eat both plants and animals.
37	Animals, in turn, are food for even bigger animals. When big animals die,
50	smaller animals eat them. Some of the animal parts rot on the ground. This
64	makes nutrients for the ground. This helps the plants to grow.
75	The food chain is very simple. Here is an example. A bear gets old and
90	dies. The body lies on the ground. The little bugs and flies find the body.
105	They eat the bear. One of the flies is caught in a spider web. The spider eats
122	the fly. Along comes a bigger insect. It eats the spider. The insect rests on
137	the lake water. A little fish snaps at the insect. The little fish eats the insect.
153	A bigger fish eats the little fish. A bear comes to the lake and catches the big
170	fish. The bear eats the big fish. The cycle starts all over again. The food
185	chain happens every day in many different ways. Every part of the food
198	chain is important.
201	

Total Words Read _____

− Errors _____

= CWPM _____

Rivers and Canals: Our Water Highways

0	In the 1700s, going from one place to another was hard. The roads
13	were not good. The roads were more like trails. People had to walk, ride
27	horses, or use horses to pull wagons. Towns were far apart. It took a long
42	time to go from place to place. It was easier to use rivers to move people
58	and goods. Rivers became very busy. Rafts moved up and down the rivers.
71	Flour, grains, cotton, wheat, corn, and meat moved on the rafts. Many
83	people used rivers to move west. They wanted farms close to the rivers.
96	There were many towns along the rivers.
103	The rivers and lakes were not connected. So people dug canals. The
115	longest canal was the Erie Canal. It was 363 miles long. It ran from the
130	Hudson River to Lake Erie. They started to dig the canal in 1819. It took six
146	years to dig the canal. Goods were placed on rafts. Mules pulled the rafts.
160	The mules walked along paths on the banks of the canals. A mule could pull
175	a load 50 times heavier than it could on any road. Now goods and people
190	could move easily.
193	

Total Words Read _____

− Errors _____

= CWPM _____

Marco Polo: A World Traveler

Marco Polo was born in 1254. He lived in Venice. He was one of the first people to travel to China. He was seventeen when he left on his trip. He went with his father. It took three years to get to China. They used camels. There were many stops along the way. They crossed mountains, rivers, and deserts.

In China, Polo saw many new things. Colorful silk cloth was used to make clothes. Food had many spices. The people ate rice and drank tea. Life was well-ordered. The cities were large. Paper money was used. Moveable print blocks were used to print on paper. Good records were kept. They had fireworks. Kites flew in the sky. A compass was used in travel. The Polos were away from home for twenty-four years. They brought back gold, silver, diamonds, and rubies.

Marco Polo wrote a book. The book was about the many things he saw and did in China. He told about life in China. At first people did not believe him. Some people went to China. They found that Marco Polo was right. Trade between China and Europe grew. It took a long time to travel to China. Soon people wanted a faster way to travel. Men began to sail to China.

Total Words Read _____
- Errors _____
= CWPM _____

Practice Passage 213

The Great Wall: One of the World's Seven Wonders

0	The Great Wall of China is one of the Seven Wonders of the World.
14	The Great Wall is very big. It is in north China. The wall goes from east to
31	west. It goes over mountains, across grasslands, and through deserts. The
42	Great Wall is more than 3,000 miles long. It is about 40 feet tall and 15 feet
59	wide. The top of the wall is more like a big road for horses and people to
76	walk on. Because the Great Wall is so big and long, it can be seen from
92	outer space
94	It took more than 2,000 years to build the Great Wall. It was built to
109	keep the enemies out of China. Along the wall are watchtowers. A long time
123	ago, soldiers and horses lived on the wall. There are big gates in the wall. In
139	times of peace, people could come and go from China.
149	There are hundreds of steps to the top of the wall. Today people can
163	climb to the top of the Great Wall. Many people come to visit the Great Wall
179	every year. They climb to the top of the wall. Some of them buy a T-shirt
195	that says, "I climbed to the top of the Great Wall." They are proud that they
211	were able to climb to the top of the wall.
221	

Total Words Read _____

− Errors _____

= CWPM _____

Practice Passage 214

The Louisiana Purchase: A Good Deal

0	The Mississippi River valley is very large. In 1800, it belonged to
12	France. All of the rivers that feed into the Mississippi are part of the valley.
27	The people of the U.S. lived on the east side of the river. They farmed the
43	land. Rivers were used to move farm goods. They floated wheat, lumber,
55	tobacco, and cotton on log rafts. New Orleans is at the end of the river.
70	Farm goods were sold in New Orleans. The goods were sent to the U.S. and
85	other ports. New Orleans belonged to France. New Orleans was a big city.
98	People wanted New Orleans to be part of the U.S.
108	In 1802, France was in a long war. France was at war with England.
122	France wanted money for the army. The U.S. was going to give ten million
136	dollars for New Orleans. France offered to sell the whole valley. Not just
149	New Orleans. The U.S. took a chance. They offered five million. France said,
162	"No." The U.S. knew the river valley was very big. In the west, it goes all of
179	the way to the Rocky Mountains. In the north, it goes almost to Canada. The
194	U.S. made a final offer of 15 million. France needed the money. They
207	accepted the offer.
210	This was a good deal for the U.S. People could move west. There was
224	lots of land for the people to farm. The U.S. became much bigger.
237	

Total Words Read _____
− Errors _____
= CWPM _____

Benjamin Franklin: Inventor and Statesman

Ben Franklin was born in Boston in 1706. His father was a soap and candle maker. He had sixteen brothers and sisters. At ten, he started to work in his father's shop. He worked for his father for two years. Then he went to work for an older brother. Ben worked for nine years in his brother's print shop. At the age of 17, he left.

Ben went to Philadelphia. He opened his own print shop. He printed a newspaper and books. He wrote *Poor Richard's Almanac.* This book was filled with advice. It had odd bits of wisdom. "Early to bed and early to rise, makes a man healthy, wealthy, and wise." "God helps them that help themselves." "One today is worth two tomorrows." "When the well is dry, they know the worth of water." He printed a new book every year. Many people bought his books. He became very rich.

Ben was an inventor. His cast-iron stove heated a room. Most of the heat did not go up the chimney. Bifocal eyeglasses let people see near and far. They did not need two pairs of glasses. He proved that lightning was electricity. To do this he flew a kite in a storm. He made a lightning rod. People put lightning rods on their houses. Lightning would strike the rod. It would travel to the ground. The house would not burn. Ben became famous.

Ben was a public servant. He helped to set up the first fire department. He worked on the first library. He was the town postmaster. He wanted to unite all of the colonies. He signed the Declaration of Independence. Ben Franklin cared about the U.S.

Weather: It's What's Outside That Counts

How do we tell the weather? We look outside. The weather is the air around us. Weather can take many forms. Rain, snow, and wind are forms of weather. Hurricanes and tornadoes are also forms of weather. Many elements work together to make weather. There are three important elements. They are heat, air, and water.

Heat comes from the sun to the earth. Without heat, there would be no life. Heat travels in the form of light and energy. When it arrives, it enters the blanket of air that surrounds the earth. This blanket of air is called the atmosphere. Atmosphere has weight. It presses down on all parts of the earth. This pressure is called air pressure. The earth's air is full of air pressure. Some parts have low pressure. Warm air is lighter than cold air. When there is warm, light air, there is lower air pressure. Other parts of the earth have high air pressure. When the air is colder, the pressure is higher.

Wind is made when air moves between low and high pressure areas. When there is a big difference in pressure, the wind moves fast. Sometimes this causes very strong winds. Strong winds cause hurricanes and tornadoes

Water is also important. Our air is made up of many gases. One kind of gas is water vapor. Water turns into water vapor when it is warm. On warm days, there is more water vapor in the air. On cold days, there is less water vapor. The amount of water vapor determines how humid the air will be. When air rises, water vapor can turn into droplets. These droplets can make clouds. Then clouds can cause water to fall from the sky.

Weather is important. It affects our lives. If the weather is nice, we like to be outside. We wear light clothes. If the weather is bad, we try to stay inside. We wear thick, warm clothes. We can't control the weather. But we need to pay attention to it.

Guide Dogs: Helpful Pets

0   Most people think of dogs as great pets. But some dogs are more than
14 pets. They are guide dogs. Guide dogs help people in many ways. Seeing
27 Eye dogs help people who are blind. These dogs act as eyes for their
41 owners. Seeing Eye dogs help their owners travel from place to place. Seeing
54 Eye dogs ride on buses with their owners. They lead people across busy
67 streets. The dogs go in stores and restaurants with their owners.

78 Hearing dogs help people who are deaf. These dogs alert their owners
90 to important sounds. Hearing dogs can be trained to listen for the telephone
103 ring. They might listen for the doorbell or alarm clock. They can also listen
117 for a baby's cry. The Hearing dog will nudge its owner when it hears an
132 important sound.

134 Other dogs are helpers for people in wheelchairs. These dogs help with
146 physical tasks. They might pick up dropped objects. They are trained to flip
159 light switches. These dogs are able to open drawers and doors.

170 Guide dogs help their owners to live full lives. With a guide dog, owners
184 don't have to rely on other people to help them. They can be independent.
198 Guide dogs are more than pets. They are lifelines for their owners.
210

Total Words Read _____
− Errors _____
= CWPM _____

Practice Passage 218

Sharks: Amazing Fish

Sharks have lived in the oceans for millions of years. Sharks were on earth before there were whales. They were on earth before the dinosaurs.

Sharks are amazing fish. They have many teeth. In fact, sharks are covered with teeth. Unlike other fish, sharks do not have bones. Most fish have skeletons made of bone. But a shark skeleton is made of gristle. Bony fish have skin that is covered with smooth scales. Sharks have skin that is covered with denticles. Denticles are small, sharp teeth. They can cut and scratch. Sharks have many rows of teeth. If a shark tooth falls out, another tooth moves forward to take its place. This happens very quickly. During its lifetime, a shark may have a thousand sets of teeth.

Many people think there is just one kind of shark. In fact, there are at least 350 kinds of sharks. The largest shark is the whale shark. It is as big as two elephants. The smallest shark is the cigar shark. It can fit in a person's hand. The great white shark is known as "the man eater." People are afraid of the great white shark. It sometimes attacks people in water. The great white shark mostly eats large fish. It also eats seals and otters.

There is no type of shark that naturally preys on humans. Only in the last 100 years have there been reports of shark attacks on people. This is because more people are going in the water. A person is more likely to be killed in a car accident than to be attacked by a shark.

Total Words Read _____
− Errors _____
= CWPM _____

Roads and Highways

Until about 1850 there were no real roads in the U.S. Most towns were near water. Roads were used to get things to docks. Rivers and canals were used to carry things long distances. Most people traveled on foot, on horses, or by horse-drawn wagons. Some people used trains and boats. Roads were trails through the woods. The trails were narrow and rutted. They were muddy when it rained. Snow piled up on the trails. Trails were dusty in the summer. Sometimes the trails had logs across them. The roads were not good.

In the 1900s, people began to own cars. People could not drive cars on the trails. They wanted good roads. In 1909, there were over 190,000 miles of road with a hard surface. These roads were made of crushed rock. They were not made of concrete. People wanted better roads.

By 1920, more people had cars. Cars saved time and work. People did not want to wait for trains and boats. They wanted to go places that trains and boats did not go to. People wanted to go lots of places in cars. People wanted more roads.

When there were better roads, people started to use buses. Trucks were a new way to carry things. By 1930, there were 640,000 miles of roads with hard surfaces. People used roads more and more. Today there are millions of miles of roads in the U.S.

Chinese Kite Flying: A National Pastime

Kites in China reflect culture. Kites have many shapes. Most of the kites are made in the shape of animals. The kite shapes that most people like are deer, tigers, birds, fish, and dragons. People in China think that the animal shapes have meaning. Deer are good luck. The tiger, king of the animals, is mighty and strong. Catfish are for more wealth in the coming year. Dragons are wise and very important in China. Many kites look like dragons. In China, there are many big and many small kites. Old and young people fly kites.

In China people have flown kites for more than 2,400 years. The old people teach the young people about kite culture. They show them how to make the kites with paper and wood. Some little kites have one part. Very big kites have many parts and shapes. The people paint the kites with many colors. The kites are very pretty. Every day many people fly kites in the sky.

People believe that kite flying is healthy. When someone is worn-out and tired, or when they want to get out of the house, they go outside and fly a kite. They watch their pretty kites go up in the sky. When people fly kites, they can look at the sky, clouds, and trees. This makes them feel good and happy. Many people in China like to fly kites.

Total Words Read _____
− Errors _____
= CWPM _____

Level 3 Practice Passages

301	White, Brown, and Black: The Bear Facts
302	Yangtze River
303	Is It a Solid, a Liquid, or a Gas?
304	Sponges: Simple Animals
305	Camels: One Hump or Two?
306	Seasons: Passages of Time
307	Whales: Huge Sea Mammals
308	Terra-Cotta Warriors
309	Bridges: An Important Beginning
310	The Right to Read
311	Helen Keller: Triumph Over Tragedy
312	The Birth of a River
313	Blackbeard: A Fierce Pirate
314	Beware of Bears
315	Sounds: Moving Waveforms
316	Bones, Bones, Bones
317	Caves: Underground Rooms
318	Glaciers: Rivers of Ice
319	The Giraffe: World's Tallest Animal
320	Cesar Chavez: Champion of Migrant Farm Workers

White, Brown, and Black: The Bear Facts

There are three types of bears in North America. They are the polar bear, the brown bear, and the black bear. Canada and Alaska are the only places where all three types of bears live.

Polar bears are marine mammals. They live in very cold climates where there is ice and snow. Polar bears have hair that looks white. They are the largest kind of bear. When they stand on their hind legs, polar bears are between 8 and 10 feet tall. Polar bears can weigh between 600 and 1,400 pounds. They are meat eaters. They have special claws which help them to hold onto the ice and catch seals. The ringed seal is the polar bear's favorite meal!

Brown bears have different colors and names. Some brown bears are dark brown. Other brown bears are blonder. All brown bears have a hump above their shoulders. This hump is made of fat and muscle. Brown bears who live on the coast are called brownies. Those who live in the interior are grizzlies. Grizzlies are smaller and meaner than brownies. Brown bears are 6 to 8 feet tall when standing on their hind legs. They can weigh between 400 and 1,500 pounds. Brown bears eat a lot of different things like bugs, fish, berries, and baby animals. They spend all summer eating to store up fat for a winter nap.

Black bears are the smallest kind of bear. They are only 5 or 6 feet when standing on their hind legs. Some black bears are a jet black color. Others are lighter. Most black bears have brown noses and big ears. Black bears weigh between 100 and 400 pounds. They have claws that are sharp and curved. These special claws help them to climb trees.

Total Words Read _____

− Errors _____

= CWPM _____

Yangtze River

0   The Yangtze River is the longest river in China. It is the third longest
14   river in the world. It runs from the mountains in the West to the flat land in
31   the East by the China Sea. Over 700 rivers flow into the Yangtze. The water
46   in the river is brown. The river runs like a zigzag all of the way from the
63   mountains to the sea.
67   The Yangtze River is divided into three parts. In the upper part, the
80   river is small. There are many big rocks and waterfalls. The water moves
93   very fast. Boats cannot sail in the upper part.
102   In the middle part, the water flow is slower. Many boats sail on the
116   river. There are tall hills on both sides of the river. Sometimes only one boat
131   can sail at a time. There are lots of trees and flowers. It is very pretty. There
148   are many small towns and fishing villages built along the river. In this part
162   of the river, a dam is being built. It will be the world's biggest dam. Then
178   there will be no more floods.
184   In the lower part of the river, the river is wide. The water flow is very
200   slow. Many ships sail on the river. The land beside the river is flat. There
215   are many farms and big cities along the river.
224   The Yangtze River is a very important river in China. People have
236   lived and worked along the river for thousands of years.
246

Total Words Read _____
− Errors _____
= CWPM _____

Is It a Solid, a Liquid, or a Gas?

Scientists tell us that all matter has three forms. All matter has some weight or mass. All matter also takes up some space in our universe. Atoms make up all matter. There are three forms of matter.

The first kind of matter is a solid. A solid has weight or mass, and it takes up space. A solid is different from a liquid or a gas. A solid has its own shape. Solids, such as wood, a glass, or a toy top, are one example of matter. Solids are hard. They don't change their shapes. Some other examples of solids are soft and bend easily. Shirts and modeling clay are two examples of this kind of solid.

The second type of matter is a liquid. Water, milk, and honey are examples of liquids. A liquid does not have a shape of its own. A liquid takes the shape of whatever container it is in. If milk is in a tall glass, then the milk is tall. If honey is on a spoon, then the honey takes the shape of the spoon.

The third type of matter is a gas. A gas is like a liquid because it takes the shape of its container. But a gas is different from a liquid in that it fills the entire container. A gas may have color or a smell, but it may not have either. We can't see the air, but we can feel it when the wind blows. Matter is what makes up our universe, and it only takes three forms. Those three forms make up everything in our world.

Total Words Read _____
− Errors _____
= CWPM _____

Practice Passage 304

Sponges: Simple Animals

Many people think of a sponge as a kitchen tool. Kitchen sponges are one kind of sponge. These sponges are man-made. Other types of sponges are alive. These types of sponges are animals. They actually look more like plants than animals. However, a sponge is the simplest form of a multicellular animal. Most sponges live in the oceans of the world. A few sponges live in fresh water. Sponges do not live on land.

There are two basic types of sponges: encrusting and freestanding. Encrusting sponges look like moss. They cover the surface of rocks. Freestanding sponges have more inner volume. They can grow into strange shapes. They can become very big. The barrel sponge is a freestanding sponge. It grows in the tropics. A whole person could fit inside some barrel sponges. Tube sponges also grow in the tropics. They come in many beautiful colors.

A sponge does not have a head or a mouth. Nor does a sponge have arms or feet. So a sponge cannot move. It stays in one place for its whole life. If a sponge is touched, it does not react. It lives on the bottom of the ocean. A sponge attaches to something solid. It finds a place where there is enough food. A sponge does not make its own food like a plant does. That is one reason that the sponge is an animal. Sponges capture food. A sponge eats tiny plants and animals that live in the water around it. Sponges have a thin outside layer. Inside this outer layer is an open space. The open space is called a pore. Tiny hairs move constantly in the water. The hairs send food and water through the pores. Special cells in the pores eat the tiny bits of food and organisms. The rest of the water and food goes out the top of the sponge. Sponges are covered with pores. No wonder that their scientific name means, "pore-bearing."

Total Words Read _____
− Errors _____
= CWPM _____

Level 3 Practice Passages

Camels: One Hump or Two?

Camels are funny looking mammals with humps on their backs. Camels are large animals. They are seven or eight feet tall. They have small heads but long, curved necks. Their legs are long, but their bodies are heavy. Camels are used for riding or for carrying heavy loads.

There are two kinds of camels. Camels with one hump live in Arabia, Asia, and North America. These camels have long legs and are good for riding. One-hump camels can run 8 or 10 miles an hour. They can travel 100 miles each day. Riding a camel is not like riding a horse. First, a camel has to kneel down before the rider can get on its back. These camels have hard pads on their knees and chest. The camel's feet are wide, with two toes. This helps to keep them from sinking into the sand. The camel moves its right legs together and then its left legs. Riding on a camel is like rolling or swaying from side to side.

Two-hump camels live in Central Asia. They are used to cold climates and rocky land. Camels with two humps have shorter legs with hard soles on their feet. They are used as pack animals. These camels can carry four- or five-hundred pounds on their backs. They can walk two or three miles an hour.

Total Words Read _____

− Errors _____

= CWPM _____

Seasons: Passages of Time

Our planet is always moving. Earth moves around the sun in a path. This path is called an orbit. Each year, the earth orbits the sun. There is an imaginary line that runs through the center of the earth. This line is called an axis. The two points where the axis passes through the earth are called poles. There is the North Pole and the South Pole. As the earth moves around the sun, it spins on its axis. This spinning causes day and night. The side of the earth that is pointed to the sun has daylight. The side of the earth that is pointed away from the sun has darkness. The days change as the earth orbits the sun. The length of the days changes. The temperature changes.

There are four seasons: fall, winter, spring, and summer. The seasons change because of the earth's axis and the earth's orbit. Each of the earth's poles is turned toward the sun for part of the year. Each pole is turned away from the sun for the other part of the year.

Fall begins in late September. The first day of fall is called the fall equinox. During the fall equinox, the sun is just above the equator. The day and the night are the same length. During the fall season, temperatures drop more quickly.

Winter begins in December. The first day of winter is called the winter solstice. It is the shortest day of the year. That means that there are less hours of daylight than on any other day of the year. After December 21, the days begin to get longer by a few minutes each day.

Spring begins around March 20. As in the fall season, there is an equinox in the spring. That is when the day and the night are the same length. After the spring equinox, the daylight hours get longer by a few minutes every day. The temperatures start to get warmer.

Summer is the warmest season. It begins around June 21. The first day of summer is called the summer solstice. It is the longest day of the year. That means that there are more daylight hours on this day than on any other day.

Total Words Read _____
- Errors _____
= CWPM _____

Practice Passage 307

Whales: Huge Sea Mammals

0	The whale is a sea mammal that breathes air but cannot live on land.
14	It is the largest known mammal. The whale is one of two kinds of mammals
29	that live in the water for their entire lives. Like all mammals, whales are
43	warm-blooded and nurse their young. There are many kinds of whales. The
56	largest whale is the blue whale. A blue whale can grow to be about 94 feet
72	long. That is the size of a 9-story building. The smallest whale is a dwarf
88	sperm whale. These whales only grow to be about eight-feet long.
100	A whale looks like a very large fish. It has flukes in its tail, which help
116	it to swim through the water. Whales have flippers that are sort of like the
131	fingers and hands of mammals that live on land. The whale is covered with
145	smooth, glossy skin, which helps it to swim fast in the water. Below the skin
160	is a layer of fat called blubber that helps to keep the whale warm. Because
175	of this blubber, a whale does not need as much hair or fur as a land
191	mammal. In fact, adult whales have almost no hair. Whales have large,
203	broad heads, but very small eyes. Whales breathe air through their lungs
215	before diving underwater for fifteen or twenty minutes at a time. While air is
229	in the whale's lungs, it becomes warm and moist. When this air is released
243	through the whale's blowhole, it becomes a kind of vapor. This is the called
257	the spout. Each type of whale has its own kind of spout. For example, the
272	blue whale has a tall, thick spout while the humpback whale's spout is low
286	and round. Experienced whale watchers can tell whales apart by their spouts.
298	

Total Words Read _____

− Errors _____

= CWPM _____

Terra-Cotta Warriors

    The first emperor of China built a big tomb. When he died, he wanted to be buried in his tomb. The tomb was very, very big. It was made of wood. It covered more than five city blocks. The emperor had a big army. He had more than 8,000 soldiers. He had more than 500 horses. A clay model was made for each of his soldiers. Clay models were made for the horses. The emperor put the clay soldiers and horses in the tomb. He put bows, arrows, and spears in the tomb.

    The emperor believed that the souls of the soldiers and horses would go to the afterlife with him. The first emperor was not nice to his people. He made them build his tomb and work on the Great Wall. The people were not happy. When the emperor died, he was put in the tomb with the clay soldiers and horses. Two years later, the poor farmers got mad. They broke into the tomb. The farmers took the bows, arrows, and spears. They knocked down the soldiers. The clay soldiers broke into pieces. The poor farmers burned the tomb. Everyone forgot about the tomb. Dirt covered the tomb. It became a little hill. People started to farm on the hill.

    Two thousand years later, in 1974, some farmers were digging a well. They found some clay parts of the soldiers. They started to dig a pit. In China, they are still digging in the pit to this day. They find parts of the clay soldiers. Then they put each soldier back together. It will take many years to dig up the soldier parts. It will take even longer to put all of the soldiers together. There may even be more clay figures in the tomb of the first emperor.

Bridges: An Important Beginning

    Bridges are important. People have many reasons to build bridges. Cave people built bridges with logs. They put logs across a stream. Then they walked to the other side. People who lived in jungles made bridges from vines. They twisted plant vines into ropes. They put two vine ropes next to each other. Then they tied the vines to trees. Bridges helped people to cross rivers. They could go to a better hunting ground. They could go to trade with other people.

    People all over the world build bridges. Bridges are made in many ways. In China, bridges were made with houses on each end. Sometimes there were places to eat on the bridges. These kinds of bridges were nice for travelers. The Romans made beautiful stone bridges. Roman bridges had rounded openings. These openings are called arches. Arch bridges are still built today. In Persia, armies built bridges that floated. They used small boats with a floor on top. Armies used floating bridges when they wanted to cross water in a hurry. Floating bridges are called pontoon bridges.

    Not all bridges go over water. Some bridges go over land. Some go over railroad tracks. Others go over buildings. Still others go over highways. Early bridges were made of wood. Now they are made of steel or concrete.

Total Words Read _____

− Errors _____

= CWPM _____

The Right to Read

Reading is important. It is a useful skill. People who can read have an easier time in life. They can read traffic signs, menus, and maps. They can pass a test to get a driver's license. They can apply for a job. Reading is also powerful. People who can read can learn about all kinds of things.

However, not everyone can read. Some experts study reading. They say that one out of every six people in the world can't read. There are many reasons for this problem. Some countries do not let girls go to school. In those countries, many women cannot read. Other people live in very poor countries. No one can afford to learn to read in these countries. They are busy trying to find food to eat. Many countries are at war. Their people are fighting to stay alive. They do not have time to learn to read.

In the U.S., there are many people who do not speak English. They came from other countries. It is hard to come to a new country. It takes time to learn the language well enough to read it. Other people have learning problems. It is harder for them to learn to read.

The good news is that everyone can learn how to read. There are special programs to teach people to read. One of the best ways to become better at reading is to read every day. Countries want to show their citizens how important it is to learn to read. Every September 8, we celebrate International Literacy Day. Literacy is a word that means being able to read, write, and speak.

Practice Passage 311

Helen Keller: Triumph Over Tragedy

0   Helen Keller was born on June 27, 1880. She was a healthy baby at
14   first. Then she got sick. She had a high fever. Helen almost died. The fever
29   went away after many days. But Helen was not the same. She was now deaf
44   and blind.
46   The next few years were very hard. Helen was angry. She cried and
59   threw things on the floor. She grabbed food off people's plates. Her parents
72   did not know what to do. They asked an expert for help. He was Alexander
87   Graham Bell. Bell had invented the telephone. But he also worked with deaf
100 children. Bell told Helen's parents to hire a special teacher for Helen.
112 Helen's parents wrote to a special school. It was the Perkins School for the
126 Blind. They asked for a special teacher to come work with Helen.
138   On March 3, 1887, Annie Sullivan came to live at the Keller's home.
151 Annie told Helen's parents that Helen must learn to behave. She said that it
165 was not fair to let Helen act wild. The kind thing to do would be to teach
182 Helen. Annie showed Helen how to eat with a spoon and fork. Most
195 important of all, Annie taught Helen words by spelling them into her hand.
208 At first, Helen did not understand. Her teacher never gave up. One day,
221 Annie poured water over Helen's hand. Then she spelled the word water
233 into Helen's hand. Finally, Helen understood! She understood that words
243 had meaning. That day was the turning point for Helen. From then on, she
257 began to learn quickly. Helen learned to read using raised letters. Later, she
270 learned to read braille. Helen also learned to write. She used a special
283 typewriter. Annie Sullivan continued to help Helen. Helen Keller went to
295 college. The college was Radcliffe College in Boston. Helen was the first deaf
307 and blind person to earn a degree from Radcliffe. The story of Helen Keller
321 and her teacher, Annie Sullivan, is a famous one. Many books, plays, and
334 movies tell their story.
338

Total Words Read _____
- Errors _____
= CWPM _____

Practice Passage 312

The Birth of a River

0	Have you ever wondered how a river begins? A river gets its start high
14	in the mountains or in the hills. It begins as a very small stream. The river
30	may also get its start from a spring bubbling from beneath the ground. The
44	little stream begins to flow downward from its mountain home. Other little
56	streams join it. More and more water begins to flow downward. Soon the
69	little streams have joined to become a brook. The brook continues to grow
82	bigger. Then the brook becomes a river.
89	Some smaller rivers that join the big river are called its tributaries. The
102	ground that the river flows over is called the riverbed. The river's banks are
116	its left and right sides. As the river travels, it picks up small stones, sticks,
131	and soil. Where the river empties into a lake or a sea is its mouth. The river
148	drops what it is carrying at its mouth when it meets a lake or the sea. All of
166	the stones, sticks, and soil the river drops build up to form land.
179	The land that is formed at the river's mouth is called its delta. The
193	river's delta has rich soil for farming. A river delta grows many crops. It
207	takes hundreds and hundreds of years to build up the river's delta.
219	Sometimes the river floods and takes soil from its delta. Other times it just
233	keeps on adding soil. This makes its delta even larger. All of the small
247	streams, brooks, and small rivers that empty into the big river form the big
261	river's basin. Some river basins are hundreds of miles wide.
271	

Total Words Read _____

− Errors _____

= CWPM _____

Level 3 Practice Passages

Blackbeard: A Fierce Pirate

Blackbeard was one of the most hated pirates of all time. He became a pirate around 1713. He is thought to have come from England. His real name was Edward Teach. He had a long, black beard that covered most of his face. He braided his long, black beard and tied the braids with hemp. He also put hemp in his hair. Then he would light the hemp during battles. Blackbeard looked like his face was circled with fire. Many people were afraid of Blackbeard. When they saw him coming, they would give him what he wanted. Then Blackbeard would let them sail away. If people tried to fight Blackbeard, he would kill them. Even Blackbeard's own men were afraid of him.

Blackbeard spent a lot of time off the coast of Virginia and the Carolinas in 1717 and 1718. His ship was called Queen Anne's Revenge. Blackbeard stole ships and held people for ransom. One day his ship ran aground near Cape Fear. The governor of North Carolina pardoned Blackbeard. But Blackbeard would not stop his pirate ways. Blackbeard had captured more than 40 ships as a pirate. He had caused the death of hundreds of people. Finally, the governor sent a ship to arrest Blackbeard. There was a huge, bloody battle. Blackbeard put up a big fight but was killed. He died with 5 bullets and more than 20 stab wounds in his body.

Total Words Read _____
− Errors _____
= CWPM _____

Practice Passage 314

Beware of Bears

0	Bears! Many people are fascinated by them. After all, who can resist a
13	stuffed, cuddly teddy bear? Bear enclosures at zoos are often a popular
25	exhibit. Watching adorable bear cubs romp brings smiles and chuckles from
36	onlookers.
37	Bears in the wild are a different story. Bears are powerful animals and
50	can kill humans. If you are a camper or a hiker, it is important to beware of
67	bears. Bear country can be a dangerous place. Knowing some bear essentials
79	can help to keep you safe.
85	First of all, never, ever try to feed a bear. Bears love garbage and are
100	easily turned into junk-food addicts. They will then be attracted to areas
113	when people gather, such as a camping ground. National parks and forests
125	often have special "bear-proof" trash cans. Campers are told to keep their
138	food locked up and put up in a tree. Bears will destroy cars and cabins in an
155	attempt to get to a food source.
162	When in bear country, make noise to let the bears know that you are
176	around. Bears like to be alone. They do not like to be surprised by people.
191	Bears will usually stay away if they hear you coming.
201	Be alert when you are in bear country. Stay away from dense brush.
214	Use a flashlight at night. Be on the lookout for bear droppings. Do not set up
230	camp if you see signs of a bear. Be especially careful if you see bear cubs.
246	You can be sure that the mother bear is near. She might attack to protect her
262	cubs. If you happen to come across a bear, do not run! Instead, back away
277	very slowly. Use bear (pepper) spray only as a last resort.
288	

Total Words Read _____

− Errors _____

= CWPM _____

Practice Passage 315

Sounds: Moving Waveforms

0	Sounds are a part of everyday life. Car horns beep. Dogs bark.
12	Children shout. Noisy jets roar across the sky. People whisper to one
24	another. There are hundreds of sounds made every day. It is easy for people
38	to tell them apart. But there are other sounds that cannot be heard by
52	people. These sounds are too high-pitched for the human ear. They are
65	called ultrasounds.
67	Sounds are produced by a certain type of motion. These motions are
79	called vibrations. Sound travels from a vibrating object to a human ear. It
92	does this by using a sound carrier. The sound carrier may be a solid, liquid,
107	or a gas. One way sound travels is through air. Sound waves make the
121	particles in the air move. One moving particle touches another particle and
133	makes that new particle move. Then that particle touches the next particle
145	and so on. If there is no sound carrier, no sound can be heard.
159	The speed of sound depends upon how it is traveling. Sound travels a
172	little faster in warmer air than it does in colder air. However, sound travels
186	much faster in water than it does in air. It travels even faster in solids such
202	as steel or aluminum. The denser the sound carrier, the faster the sound
215	travels. The speed of sound is slower than the speed of light though. That is
230	why we hear thunder after we see lightning.
238	

Total Words Read _____

− Errors _____

= CWPM _____

Bones, Bones, Bones

Bones are alive! They are made of living tissue. Calcium and phosphorous and bone cells make up bones. All of the bones in a body make up the skeleton. An infant has over a hundred and forty more bones than an adult. The baby has around three hundred and fifty bones in its body. An adult has only two hundred and six bones. What happened to over one hundred and forty bones? As a baby begins to grow and develop, some of those bones grow together. This is called fusion.

Bones are very important. They give bodies their shape. Muscles are attached to bones. The muscles allow the bones to give the body movement. People are able to run and jump because of their bones and muscles. Bones are also hard and strong. They protect the soft organs of the body. The heart, lungs, and brain are soft organs. Bones provide a protective cage around these important organs.

It is important to keep bones strong. One way to do this is to eat green vegetables and drink milk. Green vegetables and milk have calcium and phosphorous. These help keep bones strong. Strong bones help bodies to stay healthy.

Caves: Underground Rooms

A cave is a hollow room found in the earth. There are many kinds of caves. Caves are important to scientists who study early humanity. Scientists can often find the signs of early life in caves. Cave people lived in caves more than one hundred thousand years ago. The cave people left paintings on cave walls. These paintings showed the types of animals they hunted. Fossils of early plant and animal life have been discovered in caves.

One type of cave is formed when water wears away soft rock under the ground. Mammoth Cave in Kentucky is a famous United States cave. Mammoth Cave is more than 200 miles long. Some of its rooms are over fifty feet high. There are so many streams in Mammoth Cave that visitors can travel in boats. Since the cave is dark, the fish that live there do not have eyes. They do not need to see.

Another kind of cave is called a sea cave. This type of cave is formed by ocean waves pounding against cliffs. A famous sea cave, called Fingal's Cave, can be found in Scotland. Ice caves form when glaciers melt and then freeze again. Austria is the home of a famous ice cave. An ice cave called the Singing Cave can be found in Iceland. Another type of cave is a lava cave. The lava of a volcano forms a lava cave.

Total Words Read _____
− Errors _____
= CWPM _____

Practice Passage 318

Glaciers: Rivers of Ice

0	A river has a lot of water in it. Some rivers are long and wide. Other
16	rivers are short and narrow. One kind of river carries boats and people and
30	supplies to towns and cities along its banks. Another kind of river has a lot
45	of water in it. This river does not carry boats or people or supplies. It does
61	move, but it moves very, very slowly. This river is made of ice, and it has a
78	special name. This river of ice is called a glacier.
88	When snow falls in most places, it melts when the weather turns
100	warm. But there are some places that never get warm. The snow does not
114	melt. Year after year, the snow and ice sit on the tops of high, cold
129	mountains. After a time, the snow and ice become heavy and begin to slip
143	down the mountains. This glacier or river of ice may only move from one to
158	three feet per year. As the river of ice moves slowly down the mountains, its
173	bottom edge may begin to melt off. This melting is caused because the
186	bottom edge of the glacier reached lower, warmer valleys. The glacier
197	changes the soil it flows over as it moves slowly down the mountains.
210	Glaciers scrape the earth and move huge rocks and boulders in their paths.
223	They also move and push trees and anything else in their paths.
235	

Total Words Read _____

− Errors _____

= CWPM _____

Practice Passage 319

The Giraffe: World's Tallest Animal

  0   The tallest animal in the world is the giraffe. A baby giraffe is almost 6
 15 feet tall when it is born. It can then grow to be almost 18 feet tall! Because it
 33 is so tall, it takes a giraffe a long time to stand up. So, to be safe, giraffes
 51 sleep standing up. Then, if predators come after them, they are ready to run.
 65 Lions, hyenas, and wild dogs prey on giraffes. Giraffes have to be careful
 78 when they rest or bend down to drink. Sometimes, giraffes in a herd take
 92 turns resting or drinking. That way, one giraffe is always on the lookout for
106 danger. Giraffes have very good eyesight. They can spot danger a long way
119 away. Giraffes can run from danger. In fact, they are fast runners. They can
133 run up to 35 miles an hour! Giraffes can even outrun most horses. Their
147 speed helps them to outrun their enemies. They also have strong hooves
159 that they can use to kick out an enemy.
168   Giraffes have long necks but make very little noise. Scientists used to
180 think that giraffes were mute. They now know that giraffes do make noises.
193 These noises are called infrasounds. These sounds cannot be heard by
204 humans. Giraffes also have long tongues. Their tongues are between 18 and
216 21 inches long. Giraffe tongues are prehensile. That means that the tongue is
229 able to grab and hold on to objects. Giraffes need a long neck and a special
245 tongue in order to eat. The giraffe's favorite food is the thorny leaf that
259 grows on the acacia tree. Without a long neck, the giraffe could not reach
273 the tops of tall trees to eat their tender leaves. Without the tongue and long
288 lower lip, those same leaves would be hard to pick off the tree tops.
302   The giraffe's coat is covered with yellow and brown spots. Its coat
314 helps the giraffe to blend in with trees and tall grasses in the wild. No two
330 giraffes have exactly the same pattern of spots on their coats. In the wild,
344 giraffes live together in herds of 5 to 45 animals. Giraffes are quiet, peaceful
358 animals that are favorites of children all over the world.
368

Total Words Read _____

− Errors _____

= CWPM _____

Practice Passage 320

Cesar Chavez: Champion of Migrant Farm Workers

0   Cesar Chavez was born in 1927. He lived in Yuma, Arizona, with his
13 family. His grandfather had come to the U.S. from Mexico in 1880. He hoped
27 for a better life for his family. Cesar's father was a farmer. He worked hard
42 to grow crops on his own land. He also ran the general store.
55   In 1937, the Chavez family did not have enough money to pay taxes
68 on their land. So they lost their farm. The family was forced to move. The
83 family became migrant farm workers. Migrant workers follow the crops. They
94 go from place to place. Farm owners hire these workers to pick ripe fruit.
108 Migrant farm work was hard. The farmers lived in shacks. They did not have
122 running water. Some migrant workers lived in their pick-up trucks. Some
134 children had to work and did not go to school. Other children changed schools
148 many times. Cesar Chavez went to more than 30 schools in nine years.
161   Most of the farm workers spoke only Spanish. The farm owners spoke
173 only English. It was hard for them to talk to each other. Cesar saw that some
189 farm owners did not treat the workers well. The farm owners did not pay
203 well. They did not give the workers a decent place to live.
215   Cesar grew up to be a leader of migrant farm workers. He helped them
229 to learn to read and write in English. He helped them to become U.S.
243 citizens. Cesar started a farm workers union. He led a strike against the farm
257 owners. A strike is refusing to work until people do what you want. Cesar
271 made the owners work with the union. Cesar used strikes and boycotts to
284 help the workers. A boycott is when people refuse to buy something. The
297 farm owners finally agreed to pay better wages. The owners also gave
309 workers better housing. Cesar Chavez fought very hard to bring a better life
322 to migrant farm workers.
326

Total Words Read _____

− Errors _____

= CWPM _____

Level 4 Practice Passages

401	Wind: Friend or Foe?
402	The Giant Panda: The World's Best-Loved Animal
403	Blankets of Air Above Us
404	Super Waves
405	Tigers: The Largest Cats
406	The Great Wall of China: The Longest Graveyard
407	Water Bugs: Aquatic Insects
408	The Moon: Is It Really Made of Green Cheese?
409	Hummingbirds: Small and Fast
410	The Koala: Is It a Bear?
411	Bats: Flying Creatures of the Night
412	Gabriela Mistral: Teacher and Nobel Prize-Winning Author
413	Baboons: The Biggest Monkeys
414	Wilbur and Orville Wright: The Flying Brothers
415	Hurricanes: Harmful Storms
416	The Five Oceans of the World
417	The London Bridge: From England to Arizona
418	The Hopi: Native Americans of the Southwest
419	The Azores: Portuguese Islands
420	Olympic Sports: An Ancient Beginning

Wind: Friend or Foe?

Wind is moving air. The air around the earth is always moving. That is because the earth is continually spinning. When the sun heats the air, it becomes lighter. Lighter air moves more quickly. Lighter, hotter air becomes strong wind. How hot or cold the air is determines how quickly it moves. Winds are always blowing somewhere on the earth.

Wind can be a big help to us. There are many examples of how wind is helpful. Wind power pumps water from wells deep in the earth. Wind power also generates electricity. Windmills in Holland have kept the seawater from flooding low areas of the small country. Wind helps power sailboats and makes kites fly. Wind also cools us on hot, summer days.

But the wind can also be harmful. Strong winds in storms can damage buildings. Winds spinning in a tornado have destroyed parts of towns and cities. They have also killed many people. Hurricane winds form over warm waters. They blow into the land from the sea and cause great property damage and loss of life. Wind that has been warmed by forest fire becomes stronger. It blows the fire over larger areas of trees. Forest fires and their winds cause many trees to burn and many animals, houses, and people to be harmed.

We will always have wind because of the air surrounding our earth. Sometimes the wind is helpful to us. But at other times, wind can be harmful.

The Giant Panda: The World's Best-Loved Animal

The giant panda bear is a favorite of many people. Giant pandas are black and white animals. They are big and furry. They are cute and fun to watch. Pandas live in China. They live in bamboo forests. The bamboo forests grow in the mountains of southwest China.

The giant pandas eat bamboo. They only eat one kind of bamboo. This type of bamboo can suddenly grow flowers. The bamboo flowers for no reason at all. No one knows why or when the flowers will grow. It can happen anytime. The bamboo may flower once every ten years. Or it may go many more years without flowering. After the bamboo flowers, it dies. This happens all at once. Then the bamboo forests all over China die. This is very bad for the giant panda. It takes many months for the bamboo to grow again. Without bamboo, the giant pandas have no food. Many of the giant pandas die of hunger.

Only about 1,000 giant pandas live in the world. This is not a big number. Pandas are in danger. They may become extinct. That means that pandas would no longer exist. The next time the bamboo flowers, many pandas may not survive. People want to help the giant pandas. They study bamboo forests. They try to learn more about the giant panda. The people of China set aside large areas of land. This land is to grow bamboo for the giant pandas. No one can live in these areas. The Chinese people hope that they can help the giant pandas. No one wants the panda to become extinct.

Blankets of Air Above Us

Blankets on our beds help keep us warm at night. Our earth has blankets of air that do the same thing. In the atmosphere above us, there are four blankets of air that help keep us warm and safe on Earth.

The first blanket of air closest to Earth is called the troposphere. The troposphere is where we live. It contains the air we breathe and the warmth we need. The troposphere has most of our weather in it. Seventy-five percent of the atmosphere's total mass is found in this layer. It also has most of the water vapor of the atmosphere. The seasons of the earth occur in this first layer.

The second blanket of air in our atmosphere is the stratosphere. The stratosphere has a very important part that protects us. That part is the ozone layer. The ozone part of the stratosphere keeps the sun's harmful rays away from the earth. The stratosphere does not have much moisture. Therefore, it does not have many clouds. For that reason, airline pilots like to fly in the stratosphere.

The third blanket of air is the coldest layer in the atmosphere. It is called the mesosphere. Its name means "in between." The mesosphere becomes colder as its altitude increases. There are many strong winds in the mesosphere. These winds blow from west to east in the winter. In the summer, they blow from east to west.

The last layer of air around our earth is called the thermosphere. Its name means "warm place." It is the highest and the largest layer. This layer is very hot. Its temperature can be thousands and thousands of degrees. It is made up of gases. These gases have temperatures which vary. At the top of the thermosphere is where space begins.

The atmosphere of our earth is made up of these four blankets of air. Each one of them is important for life on Earth.

Total Words Read _____
− Errors _____
= CWPM _____

Practice Passage 404

Super Waves

0	When people see waves on an ocean or on a lake, they may think of
15	surfboards and wave runners. They probably don't give much thought to
26	how strong those waves are. They also may not think about the changes
39	those waves are bringing about. Every wave that comes ashore brings some
51	change with it.
54	Winds start the waves. Winds that blow across the seas make the
66	waves. The waves move across the surface of the seas until they meet the
80	land or shoreline. When the waves meet the shoreline, they may change.
92	For example, if the winds are blowing strongly, the waves will be very big.
106	The big waves come crashing into the coast and bring a lot of power with
121	them. The powerful waves continually pound the rocks on the land into
133	small pieces. They do this again and again. The smaller pieces of rock end
147	up on the floor of the ocean. The waves also take dirt and sand from one
163	shore and move it to another shoreline. The waves and the wind are
176	constantly changing the shoreline. In one place, they remove land and
187	rocks. In another, they add to the land. The winds and the waves they
201	create are powerful change forces on our shores. People try to build walls
214	and barriers to stop them, but usually the wind and the waves win the battle.
229	

Total Words Read _____

− Errors _____

= CWPM _____

Level 4 Practice Passages

Tigers: The Largest Cats

Tigers belong to the cat family. They are the biggest cats on earth. Most tigers are brown with dark stripes. Their stomachs are whitish in color. Tigers are endangered. That means that there are not many tigers left in the world.

There are five kinds of tigers found in the world today. One kind of tiger is the Bengal tiger. It can grow to be 12 feet long. The males can weigh almost 500 pounds. Bengal tigers eat mostly deer and cattle. Most Bengal tigers live in India. The white tiger is a kind of Bengal tiger. These tigers have white fur with brown or reddish strips. Wild white tigers are rare. None have been seen in the wild since the 1950s. Most white tigers are in zoos.

The Siberian is the largest of all tigers. The male Siberian can weigh as much as 660 pounds. Siberian tigers have pale orange fur. Their stripes are brown. Siberian tigers live mostly in Russia. They eat elk and wild boar. The Sumatran tiger only lives on the island of Sumatra. This island is in Indonesia. The Sumatran tiger is the smallest of all tigers. The males weigh only about 264 pounds. Sumatran tigers have coats that are darker than other tigers. They have broad, black stripes. These stripes are close together. Sometimes the stripes are doubled. The South China tiger is also a small tiger. Only 20 to 30 of these tigers exist in the wild. The rest of them live in zoos. Very little is known about these tigers. The Indochinese tiger is another kind of tiger. It is smaller than the Bengal tiger. Its fur is darker with short, narrow stripes. Many Indochinese tigers live in Thailand.

Practice Passage 406

The Great Wall of China: The Longest Graveyard

0	The Great Wall of China is the longest structure ever built. It is more
14	than 4,000 miles long and can even be seen from outer space! An ancient
28	Chinese emperor ordered the wall built to keep out enemies. That was more
41	than two thousand years ago. The emperor's soldiers rounded up people and
53	marched them off to begin work on the Great Wall. The wall was built
67	completely by hand. It took tens of thousands of people to build the Great
81	Wall. The wall was made of stone, brick, and dirt. Watchtowers and forts
94	were added every one hundred yards. The Great Wall was built to match
107	China's landscape. It stretches east to west across deserts and through
118	mountains. The wall was built to be about 30 feet high. It was also very
133	thick. The base of the wall is about 25 feet thick. At the top, it is about 15
151	feet thick. On top of the wall was a road where Chinese soldiers traveled
165	back and forth.
168	The Chinese workers had to work day and night. Most of them did not
182	have a choice. Some Chinese spent their entire lives working on the Great
195	Wall. If workers tried to run away or complain, they were buried alive. If
209	the Chinese did not work well, they were put to death. The Great Wall of
224	China is often called the "longest graveyard" because so many people died
236	while building the wall. The human cost of building this great wall was
249	tremendous.
250	

Total Words Read _____

− Errors _____

= CWPM _____

Level 4 Practice Passages

Water Bugs: Aquatic Insects

Many bugs that live in water are called water bugs. There are several kinds of water bugs. Water boatman, backswimmers, and the giant water bug are three kinds of water bugs. When water bugs are first born, they live in the water. As they grow up, water bugs leave the water to fly around at night. However, they spend their days in the water. The giant water bug is the largest of the aquatic insects. It can be almost 3 inches in length. Most water bugs are good swimmers. The water boatman got its name because its back legs were made to help it swim in the water. When a water boatman swims, it looks like a man rowing a boat. The water boatman is the most common kind of water bug. The backswimmer looks like a water boatman. However, as the name implies, backswimmers swim on their backs. The water boatman does not.

Water bugs eat other bugs and small fish. The water boatman eats very small animals and plants found in mud. Backswimmers eat dead animals that they find floating on water. Giant water bugs are able to suck the juices from a frog. Many people do not care for water bugs. Water bugs are pests. They like light and swimming pools. When people are around water bugs, they can expect a big, painful bite!

The Moon: Is It Really Made of Green Cheese?

0   There are many funny stories about the moon. Long ago, people
11   thought it was made of green cheese. They thought that because the craters
24   on the moon's surface looked like the holes found in certain cheeses. But
37   what are the facts about the moon?
44   The moon is our closest neighbor. It does have tall mountains, wide
56   flat places, and deep craters just like earth. But the moon has no
69   atmosphere. It has no water. It also has no living things. It does have a crust
85   like the earth though. It also is very hot and is probably molten deep inside.
100   The moon has gravity like earth. However, earth's gravity pull is six times
113   greater than the moon's. No wonder astronauts on the moon can leap as if
127   they were the greatest jumpers ever seen.
134   The moon experiences large temperature changes. During daytime, its
143   temperatures rise above 100 and at night they go below –100 degrees. The
156   temperature changes cause the moon's crust and rocks to crack and break
168   apart. Since there is no wind, the pieces of rock have changed over time to a
184   fine dust. This fine dust covers most of the moon's surface. The craters or
198   holes on the moon's surface are thought to have been made by meteorites
211   that crashed into it early in its history. Some of the craters are very large,
226   and others are quite small.
231   Astronauts have brought back rocks from the moon that were much
242   older than the rocks here on earth. We still have much to learn about the
257   moon, but at least we know it's not made of green cheese!
269

Total Words Read _____

–. Errors _____

= CWPM _____

Hummingbirds: Small and Fast

Hummingbirds are the smallest birds. Their average length is about 3 inches long. Sometimes people think they are large moths or butterflies. Hummingbirds have short legs that have tiny, weak feet attached to them. There are over 500 kinds of hummingbirds found in the United States.

Hummingbirds are mostly found in the eastern United States. They are not found anywhere in Europe or Asia. These tiny birds fly so fast their wings are a blur. They move their wings so fast that they can even fly backwards or upside-down. Hummingbirds can also hover over flowers. While they are hovering, they drink the flower's nectar using their long bills and their long tongues. They fly so fast that they catch insects in the air while they are flying. They also eat insects they find on flowers.

Hummingbirds make their nests on leaves or twigs. They only lay two tiny white eggs. These eggs are less than half-an-inch long. The male hummingbird has nothing to do with building the nest. The male does not help take care of the babies either. The female hummingbird is the only caregiver. She takes care of the babies in the nest for about two weeks. Then the young hummingbirds learn to fly and leave the nest for good.

Total Words Read _____
− Errors _____
= CWPM _____

The Koala: Is It a Bear?

The koala bear is a mammal found only in Australia. Koala is an Aboriginal name meaning "no drink." The koala is not a bear. Koalas are marsupials. That means they give birth to live young, then carry them in a pouch until they are grown. The baby koala, like the baby kangaroo, is called a "joey." The baby lives in the mother's pouch for about seven months and then exits the pouch in the back. It continues to live on its mother's back for another six months until it is fully grown.

The koala has a big, hairless nose and soft, thick, gray or brown fur. The fur on its belly is white. The koala looks cuddly, but it has sharp, curved claws and a strong grip. It lives in eucalyptus trees and eats the young tender branches. Koalas get their liquids from the eucalyptus leaves, so they do not drink water. They are nocturnal animals. That means they sleep during the day and are active at night. Koalas only leave their tree to go to another tree. This puts them at risk of being hit by cars that cannot see them in the dark.

Koalas are an endangered species. People are working hard to save them, but their numbers continue to decrease.

Total Words Read _____
− Errors _____
= CWPM _____

Bats: Flying Creatures of the Night

Bats are small, furry animals that look like mice. Bats are the only mammals that are able to fly. Bats have unusual body parts. The joint bones of a bat's arm and hand are very long. There is a thin piece of skin called a flying membrane between the last four digits of a bat's fingers. This flying membrane looks like a webbed hand and is used as a wing. Bats have a second piece of skin, or membrane, which connects their hand and ankle joints. A third membrane stretches between the bat's ankles and attaches to its tail. These pieces of skin stretch like an open umbrella over the bones of the bat's arms and fingers. In order to fly, bats use a type of motion called a flapping flight. A bat lifts and pushes itself up by lowering its wings down and pushing them forward. The bat stays in a horizontal position while it is flying. It almost looks like it is doing the swimming breaststroke! Bats fly mostly at night. They are guided by reflected sound waves. This navigation system is called echolocation. Bats are able to send out supersonic sounds with a pitch higher than humans can hear. When these sounds hit an object, they make an echo. The bats hear the echo and change course so that they do not have a collision.

Total Words Read _____

− Errors _____

= CWPM _____

Gabriela Mistral: Teacher and Nobel Prize-Winning Author

In 1889, Gabriela Mistral was born. She was born in Chile. Chile is a country in South America. Gabriela was not the name she was given at birth. She was named Lucila Godey Alcaya. Her mother was a teacher. As a young child, Lucila loved to read. She also loved to write and to sing.

Lucila grew up to be a teacher like her mother. Lucila was not only a teacher. She also was a writer. She wrote poems about nature. She also wrote about people. Lucila wanted to try to publish her work. She was afraid that the school officials would not like her work. Therefore, Lucila did not want to use her own name. So she chose a pen name. A pen name is a name that writers use only for their writing. They use their real names for everything else. Lucila chose the name Gabriela Mistral as her pen name.

Using her new name, Lucila won a poetry contest in Chile. Soon she became famous as Gabriela Mistral. As a teacher, Gabriela worked to improve schools in Chile and in Mexico. As a writer, she won the Nobel Prize for Literature in 1945. The Nobel Prize is a very high honor. Gabriela was the first Latin American writer to win the Nobel Prize.

Baboons: The Biggest Monkeys

Baboons are the biggest monkeys. They are sometimes called dog-faced monkeys. This is because they have heads that resemble a dog's muzzle. Baboons can be brown, black, or silver in color. They have long arms and feet. Baboons are intelligent animals that are adaptable to their environment. They are found primarily in Africa. Baboons can live to be 25 to 30 years old.

Baboons live in groups called troops. These troops are well-organized. Each member has its place. Dominant males usually rule the troop. They have two main jobs. The first job is to keep order within the troop. Baboons do not always get along with each other and often fight among themselves. The other job is to protect the troop from enemies. Jungle cats, like leopards, are the baboon's greatest enemy. The male baboons act as guards. They guard while the rest of the troop looks for food. Baboons are often on the move, looking for food. They live mostly on the ground. However, baboons are able to climb trees for safety. The baby baboons travel by holding onto their mother's fur. As they get older, the baby baboons ride on their mothers' backs.

Baboons eat insects, fruits, seed, reptiles, and rodents. Their favorite food is the scorpion. Baboons have large pouches in their cheeks. These pouches can hold almost as much food as their stomachs. They look under rocks and bushes for food. Baboons also hunt along with herds of other animals.

Baboons are social animals. One of their favorite activities is grooming. Baboons engage in mutual grooming as a way of forming social bonds. The grooming also helps to keep the baboons clean.

Total Words Read _____
− Errors _____
= CWPM _____

Wilbur and Orville Wright: The Flying Brothers

0	Wilbur and Orville Wright were the first people to fly an airplane. The
13	brothers lived in Dayton, Ohio. They built bicycles for a living. Wilbur and
26	Orville loved to design and invent new bicycles. The brothers opened their
38	own bike shop in 1892.
43	As young boys, the brothers received a flying toy from their father.
55	They became fascinated by the idea of flying. Wilbur spent his spare time
68	reading many books about flying. He thought human flight was possible.
79	Soon the brothers began to build gliders as well as bicycles. Gliders are a
93	type of plane with no engine. The Wright brothers built three gliders in all.
107	With each new glider, they learned more and more about flying. They
119	collected data on wing design. Some of the data tables they created are still
133	used today.
135	In 1903, Wilbur and Orville Wright built an airplane. This airplane was
147	different from their gliders. This airplane had an engine to power it. They
160	named this airplane "The Flyer." The first flight of an airplane was made on
174	December 17, 1903. It took place near Kitty Hawk, North Carolina. With
186	Orville as the pilot, the plane flew 120 feet. That first flight lasted only 12
201	seconds. The brothers continued to make flights with their airplanes. Each
212	time, they flew a longer time. Their fourth flight lasted fifty-nine seconds. It
226	flew for almost half a mile.
232	The Wright brothers' invention changed the world. For the first time,
243	people had access to places they had never before been able to go. They
257	could meet people in faraway places. The age of globalization began. With
269	air travel, people of different cultures could come together. They could share
281	ideas and values with one another.
287	

Total Words Read _____

− Errors _____

= CWPM _____

Practice Passage 415

Hurricanes: Harmful Storms

0   Hurricanes are violent storms. In fact, hurricanes are the most
10 destructive of all storms. Hurricane winds travel at speeds of at least 75
23 miles per hour. These storms are very large. They can measure from 300 to
37 500 miles in width. Their size and intensity makes them dangerous.
48   Hurricanes form in the late summer and early fall. They need moist air
61 and heat. As a result, hurricanes start over tropical seas. The process begins
74 when warm, moist air rises. Next, surrounding air flows toward the rising
86 air. Then water vapor from the warm air condenses. This means that it turns
100 into small drops of water. The drops of water form clouds. Heat is given off
115 during condensation. The air becomes warmer. Thunderstorms develop, and
124 the hurricane begins.
127   Hurricanes consist of spiraling winds. These winds spiral around a low
138 pressure area in the center of the storm. This area is called the "eye" of the
154 hurricane. Although winds rage around it, the eye of the hurricane is calm.
167 The sun may even be shining in the hurricane's eye.
177   Hurricanes die out when they no longer have moist air and heat. This
190 can happen if the hurricane moves over land. It can also happen if it moves
205 into a colder area. Some hurricanes last only a few hours. Others can last as
220 long as a couple of weeks. Hurricanes cannot be stopped. However, they
232 can be predicted. That way, people can be warned to get out of the
246 hurricane's path.
248

Total Words Read _____

− Errors _____

= CWPM _____

The Five Oceans of the World

There are five oceans in the world. These five oceans are really just one big ocean. The continents separate the oceans.

The Pacific Ocean is the largest. It covers almost half of the earth. The Pacific is the deepest ocean. It is also the stormiest one. The Pacific lies next to the west coast of North and South America. It is a warm ocean.

The Atlantic Ocean is the second largest. It has the most coastline. It also has the saltiest water. The Atlantic lies between Europe, Africa, and the Americas. It borders the East Coast of the U.S. It extends between the Arctic and Antarctic.

The Indian Ocean is the third largest. It is mostly south of the equator. The Indian Ocean touches four continents.

The Arctic Ocean is sometimes called the North Polar Sea. Some people consider this ocean to be part of the Atlantic. It is filled with ice. It is the smallest of the world's oceans. It is also the shallowest. The Arctic Ocean lies next to the state of Alaska.

The Antarctic Ocean is larger than the Arctic Ocean. It is sometimes called the South Polar Sea. This ocean is made up of the southern waters of three other oceans. The Antarctic surrounds the continent of Antarctica. It is filled with ice just like the Arctic Ocean.

Total Words Read _____
− Errors _____
= CWPM _____

Practice Passage 417

The London Bridge: From England to Arizona

0	The London Bridge has an interesting history. The first London Bridge
11	was built across the Thames River by the Romans in A.D. 43. It was later
26	rebuilt several times. These first London Bridges were made of wood. Fire
38	and floods caused these bridges to fall down. Finally, around 1176, a new
51	London Bridge was built out of stone. It took 33 years to build. People
65	hoped that the new London Bridge would last forever. Unfortunately, it did
77	not. As the city of London grew, the bridge was too narrow and small for
92	the added traffic. Its granite and rock began to crack and fall apart. The
106	bridge was too old and had too many problems. By the 1960s, the London
120	Bridge was starting to sink into the Thames River. The people of London
133	decided to build an entirely new London Bridge. They put the old bridge up
147	for sale.
149	An American named Robert McCulloch bought the old London Bridge.
159	He paid more than two million dollars for it. At the time, that was the most
175	money ever paid for an antique. The old London Bridge was taken apart
188	rock by rock. Each rock was numbered and packed in order. The rocks were
202	sent across the Atlantic Ocean to Arizona. There the bridge was put back
215	together again. The process took many years. This "new" London Bridge
226	was finished on October 10, 1971. It is in Lake Havasu City, Arizona.
239	

Total Words Read _____

− Errors _____

= CWPM _____

Practice Passage 418

The Hopi: Native Americans of the Southwest

0	Many hundreds of years ago, the Hopi lived in what is now Arizona.
13	These Native Americans were desert people. They lived on top of steep hills
26	with flat tops. These hills are called mesas. The Hopi built their houses out
40	of rocks covered with a plaster. The plaster was made of clay and water.
54	Then they joined their houses into villages. The Hopi villages are called
66	pueblos. When a Hopi man and woman married, they lived in the woman's
79	house. The Hopi women owned the houses in the pueblo. The Hopi men
92	had a special room that was underground. This room is called a kiva. The
106	Hopi men gathered in the kiva for special meetings. Women were only
118	allowed in the kiva on special occasions.
125	The Hopi grew beans and squash. Corn was their main food though.
137	The Hopi grew corn in many colors, not just yellow. Some of it was red,
152	blue, black, and purple. The Hopi women used the corn kernels to make a
166	kind of cornmeal pudding. Sometimes they added cactus plants to the
177	cornmeal to make it sweeter. Hopi women also used desert clay to make
190	colorful pottery.
192	The Hopi did not eat much meat. They did not hunt often because
205	there were not many animals in the desert. Occasionally, they ate turkey,
217	rabbit, antelope, or deer.
221	Today, many of the Hopi people still live in pueblos. They keep their
234	traditional ways. Other Hopi live a more modern American life.
244	

Total Words Read _____

− Errors _____

= CWPM _____

Practice Passage 419

The Azores: Portuguese Islands

0	The Azores are a group of nine islands. They are in the middle of the
15	Atlantic Ocean. The Azores are about 800 miles west of Portugal. The
27	islands belong to Portugal. The Azores were formed by volcanoes long ago.
39	They were once believed to be the lost continent of Atlantis.
50	Portuguese sailors discovered the Azores in 1427. By the middle of the
62	15th century, farmers lived on the islands. They grew crops like wheat and
75	sugar. Many ships sailed the seas during this time. They were on voyages of
89	exploration. The Azores became a stopping place for ships. Some ships were
101	returning from Asia. Others came back from Africa. Still others sailed from
113	the Americas. Many ships carried treasure like gold and jewels. Most ships
125	stopped at the islands for food and water. The Azores were soon an
138	important port of call. In times of war, the Azores were used for military
152	bases. Spain occupied them during the period from 1580 to 1640. During the
165	two World Wars, the Azores were used as naval and air bases.
177	Today, farmers still make their home on the Azore islands. They farm
189	the rich soil of the islands. They grow many crops. Sugarcane, tea, and
202	pineapples are grown there. The farmers also raise cattle and sheep. The
214	islands' mountains have grasses for the animals to eat. Meat, cheese, and
226	butter are shipped to Portugal for sale.
233	Tourists like to visit the Azores. The islands are beautiful. They have
245	many mountains with steep cliffs. The hillsides are a brilliant green. Many
257	colorful flowers decorate the landscape. Deep lakes fill extinct volcano
267	craters. Life is calm and simple on the islands. The Azores may be one of
282	the few unspoiled spots left in the world.
290	

Total Words Read _____
− Errors _____
= CWPM _____

Olympic Sports: An Ancient Beginning

0	The first Olympic games were held in 776 B.C. They ended about
12	eleven hundred years later in A.D. 393. The ancient Olympic games were
25	held once every four years to honor the Greek god Zeus. All war in Greece
40	was stopped during this time so the athletes could attend the games safely.
53	The first games had only a foot race. As time went on, more games
67	were added. The games lasted about five days and were held in June or
81	July. The games tested skills and strength. On the first day, sacrifices were
94	held to the gods. On the second day, footraces were held. The most famous
108	was the 220-yard race. Only men were in the races. Women were not
122	allowed to watch the games because the runners did not wear clothes during
135	many of the events. There was one race in which the contestants wore
148	armor however. On other days, there were wrestling and boxing matches.
159	The Olympic games were important in Greece. It was like a great
171	festival with much singing and dancing. The winners were given an olive
183	crown to wear on their heads and were invited to lots of parties. Olympic
197	winners were treated like movie and sports stars of today. Our modern
209	Olympic games began in 1896, just over one hundred years ago.
220	

Total Words Read _____

− Errors _____

= CWPM _____

Level 5 Practice Passages

501	All About Seeds
502	Bones: Living Tissue
503	Roadrunners: Full Speed Ahead!
504	Plants on the Defensive
505	Rome: A City Built on a Legend
506	Pandas: Not All Black and White
507	Chopsticks: A Chinese Invention
508	A Rock Is a Rock. Or Is It?
509	Totem Poles: Silent Storytellers
510	Bamboo: Useful Grass
511	Paint: A Splash of Color
512	Nessie: The Loch Ness Monster
513	Communities: Village, Towns, and Cities
514	Glaciers: Nature's Bulldozers
515	Martin Luther King: A Man of Peace
516	The Bald Eagle: America's National Bird
517	Are Giant Squids Really Giant?
518	The Metric System: Counting by Ten
519	Volleyball: Up and Over
520	Peter the Great: Russian Czar

Practice Passage 501

All About Seeds

Seeds are an important part of a plant. Seeds grow into new plants. Some seeds are tiny and can hardly be seen at all. Other seeds are large and stand out quite clearly, such as the pit in a peach or the seeds in a watermelon. Each seed has a covering around it called a seed coat. It is the seed coat that protects the seed inside it from any harm. Some seeds have a hard protective shell around them, like the scales on the pinecone that protect it. Other seeds are right outside in plain view, such as the tiny seeds that are on the outside surface of the strawberry.

Each seed has the same two parts regardless of where the seeds are located on a plant. The first part of the seed found inside the seed coat is the tiny plant itself. Also within the protective seed coat is food on which the tiny plant can feed. The seed does not start to grow until the conditions are right for it. When the seed begins to grow, it is called germination. For most seeds to begin germination, the right conditions usually include warmth from the sun and water. When the seed begins to grow, its roots begin to reach down in the soil to anchor it. Its stem begins to grow up to form the plant and its leaves. While the seed is growing, it feeds on the plant food that has been stored as part of the seed and protected by the seed coat.

Total Words Read _____

− Errors _____

= CWPM _____

Bones: Living Tissue

Some people do not realize that bones are alive. Bones are made of living tissue. Calcium, phosphorous, and bone cells make up our bones. Infants have about three hundred and fifty bones in their bodies. However, an adult body contains only two hundred and six bones. That means that an infant has over a hundred and forty more bones in its body than an adult. The reason for this difference is bone fusion. As infants begin to grow and develop, some of their bones fuse or grow together.

Every bone is covered with an outer layer. This layer consists of compact bone and is very hard. Inside the outer layer of bone is a softer bone. The inside layer is strong and spongy. Bone marrow is contained within the bone. The bone marrow makes blood for the body. The largest bone in the human body is the thighbone. Its length is related to the size of the person. Its length is about one fourth of a person's height. The smallest bones in the body are in the ear. There are three tiny ear bones that are only three millimeters long.

Bones are very important. The hard bones of the body make up a person's skeleton. The skeleton supports all the other systems in the body. Without bones, bodies would not have shapes. A jellyfish is an example of a body without a shape. Bones also protect the soft organs of the body. They do this by forming a protective cage around organs such as the heart, lungs, and brain. Damage to soft organs can cause serious problems. Bones also work with muscles to allow bodies to move. It is important to keep bones strong and healthy. One way to do this is to eat a sufficient amount of green vegetables and dairy products. Another way is to do plenty of weight-bearing exercise. Taking care of bones is important to overall health.

Roadrunners: Full Speed Ahead!

    Roadrunners are members of the cuckoo family. Their home is in the desert. Roadrunners are black and white in color. They have a distinct crest on the crowns of their heads. They also have long bills and very long tails. Their legs are extremely powerful. Strong legs enable roadrunners to run up to seventeen miles per hour. These birds can easily outrun a horse.

    Roadrunners need to be fast so they can catch their prey. They feed almost entirely on other animals. These include insects, scorpions, lizards, rodents, snakes, and other birds. They also chase grasshoppers. If a grasshopper tries to escape, the roadrunner can jump three or four feet into the air. The western roadrunner is famous for its ability to kill rattlesnakes. It is one of the few animals that is able to do so. Because of its lightning speed, the roadrunner can grab a rattlesnake by its tail. The roadrunner swings the rattlesnake around like a whip. It slams the rattlesnake's head into the ground until it is dead. The roadrunner then proceeds to eat the snake. It is not able to swallow the whole snake at one time though. So the roadrunner often keeps the snake dangling from its mouth, eating an inch or two at a time.

    Roadrunners rarely fly although they are able to do so. If it senses danger, the roadrunner may take to its wings. However, it is hard to keep its large body in the air for more than a few seconds. Consequently, the roadrunner prefers to walk or run.

Total Words Read _____

− Errors _____

= CWPM _____

Practice Passage 504

Plants on the Defensive

0   It seems strange that plants must defend themselves, but it is true.
12   Plants have enemies. Those enemies might be animals or insects who eat
24   plants. Other plant enemies are disease or molds that grow on plants and
37   kill them. Other elements such frost, fire, and strong winds are harmful to
50   plants. Plants have natural and interesting weapons to defend themselves
60   from enemies.
62   Poisons are one of the best ways for plants to defend themselves.
74   Many plants are poisonous when they are eaten. Plants like mountain laurel
86   make grazing animals sick. Certain mushrooms are extremely deadly if they
97   are eaten. Other plants have fruits, such as the nightshade or pokeberry,
109   that can cause illness and, in some cases, death. Some plants poison
121   livestock who may be grazing where they grow. The animals learn to leave
134   these plants alone. Other plants are poisonous to the touch. Plants like
146   poison oak and poison ivy cause skin itching.
154   Thorns, spines, and burrs protect other plants. Roses, cacti, and
164   berries have prickly ways of defending themselves. Other plants give off an
176   unpleasant smell or odor. Their bad odor discourages animals from eating
187   them. Some plants protect themselves from weather, fire, and disease. The
198   bark of many trees is a barrier against the weather and insects. Desert plants
212   have thick stems and few leaves. This helps them to store water.
224   Plants may look harmless. However, they have many different ways of
235   protecting themselves. Some of these ways are quite deadly.
244

Total Words Read _____

− Errors _____

= CWPM _____

Rome: A City Built on a Legend

A legend is a story about a person or a place. Although they are entertaining, legends are not true stories. One famous legend is about how the city of Rome was founded. In 753 B.C., as the legend goes, twin brothers were the founders of Rome. The brothers' names were Romulus and Remus. Their father was Mars, the Roman god of war. Their mother was the daughter of King Numitor. The king's brother was jealous of the baby boys. He did not want his nephews to inherit the throne. So the evil uncle put the boys in a basket and set it to sail down the Tiber River. The basket eventually washed ashore. Luckily for the boys, a friendly wolf rescued them. This wolf took good care of the babies and even fed them with her own milk. A kindly shepherd found the boys and raised them as his own.

When the brothers grew up, they decided to build a city. They wanted to honor the wolf that had rescued them as babies by dedicating the city to her. They wanted their city to be a place where orphans and homeless people could live. Unfortunately, the brothers got into an argument over where they should build the city. They also argued over which one of them would be the ruler of the city. In a fit of anger, Romulus killed Remus. Romulus then built his city on Palatine Hill. That was the spot where the wolf had found the twins. Romulus named the city Rome after himself.

Pandas: Not All Black and White

"Black and white" and "cute and adorable" are words that come to mind when most people hear the word "panda." These words describe the giant panda. The giant panda is as big as a bear and indeed resembles one. Giant pandas live in the mountains of central China. The Chinese name for the giant panda literally means "white bear." Giant pandas are about the same size as the American black bear. There are important differences though. Giant pandas do not hibernate, nor are they able to walk on their hind legs as black bears do. Pandas have strong teeth and jaws that are useful for chewing bamboo. Giant pandas have unusual front paws. There is a pad on each front paw. Giant pandas use these pads like thumbs to pick up food and feed themselves. These "thumbs" help the giant pandas to grab huge bamboo stalks. The giant panda is a rare mammal. Giant pandas are small at birth. But by the time they are one year old, they can weigh 60 pounds. In about five years, the giant panda is full-grown and can weigh as much as 300 pounds!

Many people are surprised to learn that there is a lesser panda. The lesser panda is different in appearance from the giant panda. The lesser panda is considerably smaller, about the size of a house cat. Its body is covered with long, thick rust-colored fur. The lesser panda has a white face with dark strips from the eye to the corner of the mouth. The lesser panda has a striped tail like a raccoon. However, both types of panda feed on bamboo shoots, climb trees, and have friendly dispositions!

Total Words Read _____

− Errors _____

= CWPM _____

Practice Passage 507

Chopsticks: A Chinese Invention

Chopsticks were invented in China more than 5,000 years ago. Long ago, food was chopped into little pieces so it would cook faster. The faster food cooked, the more fuel it would save. Since food was eaten in small pieces, there was no need for knives. Rather, chopsticks were used to move food from the plate to the mouth. Confucius was a Chinese philosopher. He was a vegetarian. It is believed that Confucius did not like knives. Knives reminded him of the slaughterhouse. He favored chopsticks. By A.D. 500, the use of chopsticks had spread to other countries. The people in present day Vietnam, Korea, and Japan, as well as China, use chopsticks today.

Chinese chopsticks are about 9 or 10 inches long. They are square at the top, have a blunt end, and are thinner on the bottom. The Chinese call them *kuai-ai*. This means "quick little fellows." Chopsticks have been made of many materials. Bamboo is a popular choice since it is available and inexpensive. Bamboo is also heat resistant. Other types of wood such as sandalwood, cedar, and teak have also been used. Long ago, rich people had chopsticks made from jade, gold, or silver. In the days of the Chinese dynasty, silver chopsticks were used. People believed that silver would turn black if it touched poisoned food. We know now that silver will not react to poison. It sometimes changes color if it touches rotten eggs, garlic, or onions.

Total Words Read _____
− Errors _____
= CWPM _____

A Rock Is a Rock. Or Is It?

All rocks might look alike, but they are quite different. Scientists have identified three groups of rocks. Rocks are made of different kinds of minerals. However, it is not the kinds of minerals they are made of that determine what group they are in. How the rock was formed determines its group. Deep down in the center of the earth, molten rock or magma flows because it is so very hot. When some of this molten magma comes closer to the earth's surface, it begins to cool and harden. This is how the first type of rock is formed. Rocks that are formed from cooled magma are called igneous rocks.

The earth is constantly moving beneath its surface with a great deal of heat and pressure. When rock that already has been formed is subjected to this heat and pressure, metamorphic rock is formed. The earth takes one kind of rock and, because of heat and pressure, changes it into another type of rock. The third type of rock also takes older rocks and forms new rocks. When plants die, their remains form layers in the earth. When animals die, their remains also form in layers. These remains are worn down by weather and climate. Over time, the layers of older rock, and plant and animal remains harden into the third type of rock called sedimentary rock. The next time you see a rock, try to figure out which type of rock it is: an igneous rock, a metamorphic rock, or a sedimentary rock.

Totem Poles: Silent Storytellers

Totem poles are a beautiful, ancient art form. They also had an important purpose. Long ago, written language did not exist. Many native tribes relied on totem poles to tell a clan's history. In Alaska, natives carved totem poles from huge cedar trees. They used animals in the region to tell their stories. The raven was one of these animals. He can be identified on the poles by his long, straight beak. The raven is thought to be able to change into many forms. He is a symbol of God. The eagle is another animal seen on totem poles. Unlike the raven, the eagle has a curved beak. To the native Alaskans, the eagle was a symbol of peace and friendship. The orca, or killer whale, was also carved on totem poles. The killer whale could be identified by sharp teeth and a dorsal fin. Other animals seen on Alaskan totem poles are the beaver, the bear, and the wolf. The beaver has a long flat tail and two big front teeth. The wolf can be distinguished from a bear on the totem pole by a longer nose and sharper teeth.

Totem poles were painted with natural resources. For example, native Alaskans used salmon eggs, minerals, and vegetables. The main colors were black, white, and red-brown. Depending on the tribe, blue, blue-green, and yellow were used as well. Totem poles often stood for 50 to 60 years. When a totem pole became rotten and fell to the ground, it was either left to decay or used for firewood.

Total Words Read _____
− Errors _____
= CWPM _____

Bamboo: Useful Grass

Bamboo is a useful plant in many places in the world. It is a type of grass that can grow to be very tall. Bamboo has stems that can reach almost 120 feet tall. This kind of bamboo seems more like a tall tree than a grass. Bamboo can be found in both the Eastern and Western hemispheres. It grows best in warm, tropical climates. Some types of bamboo can live in colder climates such as in Japan. They also grow in parts of North and South America. A smaller type of bamboo, canebrakes, grows in the southern United States swamplands.

The stem of the bamboo plant is the most useful part. Bamboo stems are hollow, smooth, and very light in weight. They are sawed into parts and used as building materials. The hollowness of the bamboo stem is useful for making water drainpipes. Bamboo is also used to make wind instruments, baskets, and containers. Some homes are decorated with bamboo furniture. Bamboo is also used to make buckets, bridges, fishing poles, and even paper. Some people even weave mats and rugs from bamboo. In some parts of the world, bamboo seeds and new stems are used for food. The shoots of some kinds of bamboo can be cooked like asparagus spears. They can also be preserved in sugar or eaten pickled. Cattle eat the leaves of the bamboo tree. As a building material, decoration, and food source, bamboo is truly a useful plant.

Paint: A Splash of Color

0	Paint has been used throughout history. In prehistoric times, people
10	painted on cave walls. While cave painting was decorative, it was also used
23	as a means of expression. Paint was later used to illustrate religious books.
36	Easel painting was created at the beginning of the Renaissance Period.
47	Paint comes in many colors. It can be used as an expression of art or
62	to protect a surface like a wall. The color of paint is due to its pigment.
78	Pigment is a dry, colored powder that is mixed with a liquid. The liquid is
93	called the vehicle. Pigment is found on the bottom of a container of paint.
107	The vehicle, usually clear, can be seen at the top. The kind of vehicle used
122	is what makes paints different from one another.
130	Water paints rely on the caking of the pigment powder to make it stick
144	to a painted surface. Sometimes glue or paste is added to paint. This helps
158	improve the ability of the paint to adhere to a surface. Water is added to
173	latex paint to separate particles of latex rubber. The particles stick together
185	when the water evaporates. Latex paint can be washed out of rollers and
198	brushes with soap and water before it dries. If the paint dries though, it is
213	much harder to clean. Chemicals are needed to remove it. Oil paints last
226	longer and give more surface protection than other kinds of paints. Linseed
238	oil is used as the vehicle for oil paints. The linseed oil works with oxygen to
254	make a tough, waterproof seal. Oil paints are too thick to apply with a
268	brush, so thinner has to be used.
275	

Total Words Read _____

− Errors _____

= CWPM _____

Practice Passage 512

Nessie: The Loch Ness Monster

   0   Loch Ness is a big, deep lake in Scotland. It has many fish swimming
 14 in it. But Loch Ness also has something else swimming in it. According to
 28 local legend, there is a monster swimming in the lake. The Loch Ness
 41 monster is nicknamed "Nessie." For hundreds of years, Nessie has been the
 53 subject of various sightings. Nessie does not resemble any other creature
 64 that has been sighted. People who have seen Nessie report that the monster
 77 has a large body and a long neck. Scientists at first did not believe that the
 93 Loch Ness monster existed. However, enough evidence was gathered to
103 prove that something unusual is in the lake!
111   A small team of scientists took sound and photographic equipment to
122 the lake. They lowered the equipment in the lake, looking for Nessie. The
135 team took pictures of what appeared to be two large creatures. The creatures
148 had large bodies and long necks. The creatures also appeared to have eyes,
161 a mouth, and stalks with nostrils at their ends. This first team felt there
175 might be as many as thirty Loch Ness monsters in the deep lake. A larger
190 scientific team began another search for Nessie. This team had underwater
201 television cameras with better sound equipment. The first two tries were
212 disappointing. The Loch Ness was dark and cloudy, so not much could be
225 seen. However, science has not given up on finding Nessie. Perhaps one day
238 the true secret of the Loch Ness monster will be revealed!
249

Total Words Read _____

− Errors _____

= CWPM _____

Practice Passage 513

Communities: Villages, Towns, and Cities

0   A community is formed when people live together in one place. There
12   are basically three kinds of communities. There are villages, towns, and
23   cities. One of the most important differences between them is their
34   populations.

35   A village is the smallest community. Most villages are farming
45   communities. There might be one or two stores in a village. A village does
59   not have a police department or fire department. It must rely on the closest
73   town or city for those services. If a village has its own school, it is small.

89   A town is larger than a village, but not as large as a city. A town might
106   be a suburb of a larger city. A town may have a few thousand people living
122   in it. It may have a downtown with a small shopping area. Towns usually
136   have a small police force and school system also. Sometimes towns have
148   their own hospitals.

151   Cities are the largest kind of community. They have always been
162   centers of activity. Some cities started as centers for religion. Other cities
174   started as centers of government. Cities may be financial centers. They can
186   also be manufacturing centers. Some cities are cultural centers. Cities have
197   many more people than towns. They have more services for their citizens.
209   Cities have their own fire and police departments. They have hospitals and
221   school systems. Cities have many types of housing available and several
232   shopping areas.

234   People choose to live in villages, towns, or cities for specific reasons.
246   One reason might be the types of jobs they have. Another reason might be
260   the needs of their families. Still others choose a place to live based on the
275   services available. People select to live in the community that best suits
287   their needs.
289

Total Words Read _____
− Errors _____
= CWPM _____

Glaciers: Nature's Bulldozers

The word "glacier" paints a vivid picture in the minds of most people. The word "glacier" comes from French and Latin roots. "Glace" is a French word meaning ice. The word can also refer to something coated with a sugar glaze. It is not hard to imagine a glacier as "sugar-coated ice."

A glacier could better be described as a river of ice. In fact, a glacier is a huge, slow-moving mass of ice nestled between mountains. Glaciers are formed when more snow falls than melts in the mountains. As snowflakes fall, they are changed into snow. When more snow is added, the old snow becomes compacted. That means that it becomes smooth and rounded. Eventually, the old snow turns into ice. This cycle occurs again and again until finally a solid mass of ice is created. The ice becomes so thick that it overflows, slides downhill, and becomes a glacier.

Glaciers are powerful forces of nature. As glaciers move downhill, grinding their way to the sea, they flatten everything in their way. Glaciers even pull small rocks along with them. These rocks scrape and scratch the ground as they are pulled along. The rocks rub against one another and eventually are ground into a fine dust-like powder which is called glacial silt. Moving rocks and soil as they travel, glaciers sculpt the landscape, carving mountain valleys or shaping peaks. It is easy to see why glaciers are considered to be nature's bulldozers.

Martin Luther King: A Man of Peace

0   Martin Luther King, Jr. was a great African American leader. He was
12   born on January 15, 1929. When he was a boy, black people did not have
27   the same rights as white people. Black children and white children went to
40   different schools. They drank from different water faucets. They ate in
51   different restaurants. Separating black and white people was called
60   "segregation."
61   Martin Luther King grew up to become a minister. In 1954, he was
74   working in Montgomery, Alabama. He wanted to change the segregation
84   laws. In 1955, a black woman named Rosa Parks was riding a bus home
98   from work. The bus driver told her to give her seat to a white person. Mrs.
114 Parks refused. She was arrested and put in jail. This made the black people
128 in Montgomery very angry. They decided to boycott the buses until the
140 segregation laws were changed. Martin Luther King helped to lead the
151 protest. After one year, the unfair law was changed. Dr. King believed in
164 peaceful protest. He did not believe in violence. When Dr. King gave a
177 speech, many people came to listen. Dr. King is famous for his "I Have a
192 Dream" speech. In this speech, Dr. King talked about a world where his
205 children would not be judged by the color of their skin. Martin Luther King
219 was awarded the Nobel Peace Prize in 1964. Unfortunately, this man of
231 peace was shot and killed in 1968 at the age of 39. He is honored every year
248 in January when the nation celebrates his birthday.
256

Total Words Read _____
− Errors _____
= CWPM _____

Practice Passage 516

The Bald Eagle: America's National Bird

The bald eagle is America's national bird. It is the emblem or symbol that stands for America. The bald eagle was chosen to represent America on June 20, 1782. This was the date when the great seal of America was adopted.

The bald eagle was chosen as America's emblem for many reasons. The eagle represents the spirit of freedom. It soars high above the mountains, living a life of freedom. It also stands for a long life. Wild bald eagles can live as long as thirty years. Once an eagle is paired with its mate, the pair will stay together until one of them dies. Pairs of eagles build nests out of sticks on the tops of very tall trees. The bald eagle has a majestic look as well. It is a big and powerful bird. It was named at a time when the word bald meant white or streaked with white. So, the bald eagle is not bald at all. Rather, the adult eagle's head is covered with white feathers. Its tail is also white. The bald eagle's body and wings are dark brown and its eyes, beak, and feet are yellow. The bald eagle was also selected as America's symbol because it is the only eagle confined to the North American continent.

One story suggests that during one of the first battles of the Revolutionary War, bald eagles were circling above the fighting men. The eagles were making shrieking cries. The patriots thought that the eagles were encouraging them by crying for freedom!

Total Words Read _____
− Errors _____
= CWPM _____

Level 5 Practice Passages

Are Giant Squids Really Giant?

In one scary movie, a giant squid attacks a diver. In another movie, a giant squid even attacks a submarine and manages to move it around underwater. Do these giant creatures exist only in Hollywood? Actually, the giant squid really is a sea animal. The giant squid is large, but not as large as it is portrayed in the movies.

Strangely enough, the giant squid is related to the small clam and the small snail. A squid, a clam, and a snail all belong to the mollusk family. The members of the mollusk family all have one thing in common. They all have a hard shell. This hard shell is to protect their soft bodies. A clam's shell surrounds its soft body and can be easily seen. The snail's shell, too, is easily visible.

But where is the giant squid's shell? The shell that protects the squid is inside its body. Instead of having one "foot" for movement like the snail or clam, the squid's foot has been divided into eight tentacles. Those tentacles have suckers for grabbing and holding food. The tentacles can be as long as twenty-two feet. The squid's body can be over thirty feet long. A large sea animal covered with tentacles reaching out to grab food can be a frightening sight. No wonder Hollywood has used the giant squid as a popular feature in horror movies.

The Metric System: Counting by Ten

More than two hundred years ago in France, a group of scientists invented a new system of measurement. They wanted the new system to be more exact than the old way of measuring. So the scientists figured out the distance between the North Pole and the equator. Then they divided this distance into ten million parts. Each part became one unit of length. This unit was called a meter. It was named after the Greek word, meter, that means to measure. The new system of measuring was named the metric system. A meter is a little bit longer than a yard.

In the metric system, the other units for measuring and weighing were based on the meter. The gram, a word that means "small weight," became the basic unit to measure weight. A gram is very small! It takes 28 grams to equal only one ounce. The liter, named after another Greek word, became the basic unit for measuring the amount of liquid in a container. A liter is equal to about 33 ounces. It is a little more than a quart. Our system of measuring is a little confusing. We have many different names and numbers that we have to remember. But in the metric system, there are only a few names. And there is really only one number: ten. The three main units in the metric system—the meter, the gram, and the liter—are changed to larger or smaller units by multiplying or dividing by ten.

Practice Passage 519

Volleyball: Up and Over

A man named William Morgan invented the game of volleyball in 1895. Morgan was a physical education teacher in a Massachusetts YMCA. He was interested in a game that would require less effort than basketball. He also wanted a game in which opponents did not come into physical contact.

Morgan designed a team game that consisted of the tapping of a ball back and forth across a net. Morgan's game is one in which teams are on opposite sides of the net. In volleyball, the players do not move around too much. Once an indoor game, volleyball later became popular as an outside game as well. It is played worldwide today.

Volleyball is played on a field or a court that is divided by a net. There are six players on each team. Three of the players play in the front, close to the net, and three play in the back. The volleyball is a rubber ball covered in leather. To begin the game, the ball is served by the player who stands at the right back of the volleyball court. The ball must go over the net without first touching the ground, another player, or the net. After the serve, the ball is tapped back and forth across the net by each team until one team is unable to return a ball. The ball must be tapped or batted by hand and may not be lifted or pushed. If the serving team fails to serve fairly or fails to return a serve successfully, it loses the serve. If the defending team fails to return a serve, then the serving team scores a point. The game is won when one team scores fifteen points.

Total Words Read _____
− Errors _____
= CWPM _____

Peter the Great: Russian Czar

Peter was born on May 30, 1672, in Moscow. When he was only 17 years old, he became the king of Russia. Russian kings were called czars. At this time, Russia was a very backward country. Peter decided to travel to Europe to learn how to make Russia a more modern country. He visited countries like England and Holland. Peter brought back western ideas to share with the Russian people. He introduced the European calendar and alphabet to his countrymen. He also shared new ideas about government, schools, and even clothes with the Russian people. Peter built a new city in Russia and named it St. Petersburg. St. Petersburg was modeled after some of the European cities Peter had visited. Peter the Great was also a strong military leader. He was interested in ships. He even built his own ship at the age of sixteen. A Russian navy was created during his reign. He won land on the Baltic Sea so Russia would have a place to dock her ships. Peter also made the Russian army stronger. Peter the Great was a popular leader with young Russians. His popularity made it possible for him to do what he wanted without being overthrown. Some historians think that Peter the Great was a wonderful leader. They give him credit for making Russia a more modern country.

Other historians do not think that Peter the Great was so great. They point out that Peter was a cruel leader. He tried to control the Russian Orthodox Church. He raided the church treasury. Peter forced the older Russian men to cut off their beards against church wishes. He made the men in his court dress like Europeans and smoke pipes. Peter forced Russian serfs, or slaves, to work in factories. Nevertheless, Peter the Great is considered a national hero in Russia. The many monuments that were built to honor him are still maintained.

Total Words Read _____

− Errors _____

= CWPM _____

Level 6 Practice Passages

601	Water: What Would We Do Without It?
602	Granite: It's More Than Just a Rock
603	The Road to Freedom: America's Journey
604	The Great Lakes: North America's Freshwater Lakes
605	Organizing Our Planet
606	Bats: Misunderstood Mammals
607	The Printing Press
608	Klondike Gold Rush: A Tale of Two Trails
609	Cells: Basic Units of Life
610	Salmon: Uphill Fighters
611	The Constitution: America's Most Important Document
612	Leonardo da Vinci
613	All That Glitters Might Be Gold
614	Zeus: Father of the Greek Gods
615	King Salmon and Friends
616	Alexander Graham Bell: Telephone Inventor
617	The Thermometer: A Measure of Many Things
618	Balance of Power: Three Branches of Government
619	Sequoya: Inventor of the Cherokee Alphabet
620	George Washington: America's First President

Practice Passage 601

Water: What Would We Do Without It?

Water is necessary for life. In fact, most living things are made of water. Also, most living things need water to survive. Although the earth is almost 70 percent water, most of the earth's water supply is frozen. Much of the earth's water can be found at both the North Pole and the South Pole. Water frozen in glaciers also contains a good deal of the earth's water. Other water can be found in numerous lakes and rivers throughout the world. Some of our earth's water supply is also found underground and must be drilled for in water wells. Water is returned to the earth by a cycle of precipitation followed by evaporation by the sun.

On average, people in the U.S. use about 100 gallons of water a day. We use water as a part of our daily lives in numerous ways. We drink it, bathe in it, and brush our teeth with it. We cook and clean with water. Some of us swim in water or travel on it. Although we use water over and over again, this does not mean we should take it for granted. It is important that we conserve water in any way that we can. There are many things we can do to save water. We should avoid letting water run down the drain as we brush our teeth, wash our hands, or rinse dishes. We can save more than 5 gallons a day by turning off the water when brushing our teeth. We could rinse dishes in a sink partly filled with clean water rather than under running water. Taking a quick shower instead of a bath can save an average of 20 gallons of water. Checking for and fixing dripping faucets and leaky toilets can save as much as 10 gallons of water per person a day. Outside, we can limit how much we water plants and lawns. We can wash our cars with a bucket of soapy water and stop the hose between rinses. Since water is necessary for our survival, water conservation efforts should be taken seriously. Conserving the earth's water supply is everyone's job.

Total Words Read _____

− Errors _____

= CWPM _____

Practice Passage 602

Granite: It's More Than Just a Rock

0	Granite is an unusual and unique kind of rock. However, granite is
12	also common and found in many places. Oftentimes, we may be surrounded
24	by granite. Mountains composed of granite stand out against the sky. Many
36	of the tallest buildings and famous statues in the United States are made of
50	granite. Granite is a special kind of rock called an igneous rock. That means
64	granite was once found in a hot liquid form called magma in the middle of
79	the earth. When the magma moved to the earth's surface, it cooled and
92	hardened. Some of that hardened rock became granite.
100	The word "granite" was derived from a word meaning "grained."
110	Granite is a strong and rough rock. Granite is mostly made of two minerals:
124	feldspar and quartz. It is the quartz in granite that gives it its sparkle.
138	Granite must be polished to smooth out its rough surface. When it is
151	polished, it shines and displays beautiful colors. Various hues of pink, red,
163	brown, black, green, and even blue can be found in granite. Because it is
177	such a strong rock, granite is used on the walls and floors of many
191	buildings. Granite is the perfect choice for monuments and statues because
202	sun, wind, and other weather will not erode it.
211	To obtain the large pieces of granite necessary for buildings, the sides
223	of mountains are sliced off in large sheets. These sheets of granite are
236	subsequently cut into thinner slices and polished for decorative uses, like
247	walls and kitchen countertops. It is amazing to think that pieces of tall,
260	rough mountains can become the shiny, bright, colorful walls on some of
272	the nation's most beautiful buildings.
277	

Total Words Read _____

− Errors _____

= CWPM _____

Practice Passage 603

The Road to Freedom: America's Journey

English people came to North America looking for a new life. They found a new land with people living on it. These people were the Native Americans. The English decided to live in America also. So they started a colony in Virginia. They named it Jamestown. Jamestown was the first permanent English colony. It was founded in 1607. Other English people came to America, too. Some of these people were called Pilgrims. They arrived on a ship called the Mayflower. The Pilgrims agreed to set up a government. They promised to obey the laws of their government. This agreement was the Mayflower Compact. It was signed on November 11, 1620.

Many other people came to America. Soon there were 13 colonies of people. However, there were serious problems. The king of England wanted the colonists to pay new taxes. The colonists did not want to pay these taxes. By the 1760s, colonists were very angry with England. They thought the taxes were unfair. They started to fight back. The colonists stopped buying English products. On December 16, 1773, colonists led a protest in Boston. They did not like a new tax on tea. So a group of colonists dressed as Native Americans. They boarded an English ship. Once on board, the colonists dumped tea into the harbor. This protest was called the Boston Tea Party.

Soon after the Boston Tea Party, the colonists and England went to war. This war was the American Revolution. The colonists won the war. They won the right to be free from England's control. They were able to have their own country. On July 4, 1776, the colonists declared their independence from England. The Fourth of July is America's birthday. It has been an important holiday for more than 200 years.

Total Words Read _____

− Errors _____

= CWPM _____

The Great Lakes: North America's Freshwater Lakes

0	The Great Lakes are important natural resources. They make up the
11	largest system of fresh, surface water on earth. There are five great lakes,
24	which are bordered by Canada and seven U.S. states. Lake Superior is the
37	deepest and coldest lake. It has the most volume of water. It is shaped like a
53	wolf's head. The land around Lake Superior has many forests but not many
66	people live there.
69	Lake Michigan is the second largest lake. It is the only one that lies
83	within the boundaries of the United States. The northern part of Lake
95	Michigan drains into Green Bay. There are fisheries in Green Bay. There are
108	also waste products from paper mills. The southern part of Lake Michigan
120	has many people. The metropolitan areas of Milwaukee and Chicago are
131	located near Lake Michigan.
135	Lake Huron is the third largest lake. It is surrounded by sandy shores.
148	People like to visit it. There are summer cottages along the shores of Lake
162	Huron. Like Lake Michigan, Lake Huron also has a productive fishery. Lake
174	Erie is the smallest of the lakes in volume, as well as the shallowest. Because
189	it is shallow, Erie is also the warmest of the five lakes. There are many city
205	areas around the Lake Erie basin. The land around Land Erie has fertile soil.
219	Lake Erie is the lake most exposed to the effects of city life and farming. From
235	the air, Lakes Michigan, Huron, and Erie resemble the shape of a mitten.
248	The smallest lake in terms of area is Lake Ontario. It is deeper than its
263	neighbor, Lake Erie, though. The cities of Toronto and Hamilton are located
275	around Lake Ontario. These five great lakes cover more than 94,000 square
287	miles. They hold almost one-fifth of the world's supply of fresh surface water.
301	The United States obtains almost all of its fresh water supply from the Great
315	Lakes. North America's freshwater lakes are important natural resources.
324	

Total Words Read _____

− Errors _____

= CWPM _____

Organizing Our Planet

Humans have always tried to organize the world in which they live. Plants and animals have been named since the beginning of time. Aristotle tried to organize the living world over 2,000 years ago. He formed two groups. Living things were either plants or animals. He then further grouped the animals by where they lived. There were animals that lived on land, in the water, or in the air. He classified plants into three groups. Plants, according to Aristotle, were trees, shrubs, or herbs.

Over time, many other ways to organize living things were tried. They all failed because of language differences and lack of knowledge about the plants and animals. For example, a starfish is not a fish. A horseshoe crab should really be called a horseshoe spider. Depending on where one lives, a mountain lion may also be called a puma or a cougar.

Finally, a Swedish scientist named Carl von Linne devised a grouping system. He decided to use Latin to name the groups. Latin was no longer used as an oral language, so it wouldn't change over time. He liked Latin so much that he even changed his own name to a Latin version of von Linne. His name became Carolus Linnaeus. Linnaeus studied thousands and thousands of plants and animals. He decided to group the plants and animals by their structures. His classification system is used today by scientists all over the world to place plants and animals into similar groups.

Bats: Misunderstood Mammals

Bats are perhaps the most misunderstood of all the mammals. For example, the expression "blind as a bat" is widely used. The supposition that bats are blind is just one of the many misconceptions about these flying mammals. In reality, bats are not blind at all. In fact, while all bats can see, many bats can even see better than some people. There are basically two kinds of bats—large and small. Mega bats have excellent eyesight. Their large eyes enable them to see fruits and flowers in the night. Smaller bats rely on echolocation while flying at night, but even these bats are able to see. The echolocation assists them in finding insects. Most bats have better night vision than day vision, however.

Many people think of bats as vampires that suck people's blood. There are nearly 1,000 species of bats in the world. They live in almost all areas of the world except for the very cold regions like Antarctica. Only three species of bats, those living in Mexico and South America, eat the blood of mammals and birds. Even these bats do not suck the blood. Instead, they make a small bite in the animal's skin using their very sharp teeth. They then lick up the blood. Bat saliva has a chemical that prevents blood from clotting before the bat is finished eating. Scientists are studying bats to see if this chemical could prevent human strokes caused by blood clots.

Bats are important to humans in other ways. They pollinate trees and flowers and spread seeds so that plants grow in other areas. Bats can eat half of their weight in insects each night. Therefore, they are very effective controllers of pests who harm crops and spread disease. These misunderstood mammals are actually very valuable creatures.

Practice Passage 607

The Printing Press

0	Imagine having to copy an entire book by hand. That's what people
12	had to do before the printing press was invented. Books sometimes took
24	years to copy. They were very rare and extremely expensive. Monks spent
36	their entire lives just making one copy of the Bible.
46	In the early fifteenth century, a German named Johann Gutenberg had
57	a wonderful idea. He thought of a way to print books instead of copying
71	them by hand. Gutenberg took small blocks of wood and made them all the
85	same size. He then took each block of wood and carved one letter of the
100	alphabet on it. When Gutenberg wanted to print a word, he would line up
114	the blocks with the letters that would spell that word. He would spread ink
128	on each of the letters and then press them down on a piece of parchment
143	paper. He could use the same alphabet letter blocks over and over again, as
157	he strung the blocks together to make words. This method still took a great
171	deal of time, but then Gutenberg thought of a way to design a machine that
186	would print an entire page at one time.
194	Gutenberg invented that printing machine, called the printing press, in
204	1448. He printed three hundred Bibles in Latin, the language of the church
217	at the time. Forty of those 300 Bibles still exist today. They are called the
232	Gutenberg Bibles, and they are worth millions and millions of dollars. The
244	next time you pick up a book to read, imagine how long it would take to
260	print just one page if you had to line up blocks of wood letters before it
276	could be printed.
279	

Total Words Read _____

− Errors _____

= CWPM _____

Klondike Gold Rush: A Tale of Two Trails

Between 1896 and 1900, nearly 100,000 people rushed to Alaska and the Yukon Territory. The reason? Gold, of course! The word that gold had been discovered in the Yukon River traveled quickly across the United States. People from all walks of life set out to find their fortune. Unfortunately, gold-seeking was a dangerous undertaking. It is estimated that only 40,000 of the 100,000 actually made the trip to the Dawson gold fields. Once there, only 10 percent of them found gold.

Gold seekers had two choices to get to the Dawson Chilkoot and the White Pass. The Chilkoot Pass was too steep for horses, so men who could not afford horses often took this trail. The Canadian Mounties required that each miner bring a year's worth of supplies. A year's worth of supplies could weigh as much as one ton. Without these supplies, miners were not allowed to cross. Consequently, gold seekers had to strap heavy packs on their backs and drag loaded dog sleds and canoes as they hiked along. It took the men many backbreaking trips over the pass to haul their supplies. Once over the pass, miners had to build boats and travel down rushing rapids to finally reach the gold fields. Many men turned back along the way.

The White Pass trail was the other route to the gold fields. Since the White Pass was not as steep as the Chilkoot Pass trail, pack animals were allowed on this trail. Sadly, the trail proved to be too much for these animals to bear. Three thousand animals died and were abandoned along this trail. The White Pass became known as Dead Horse Trail.

Practice Passage 609

Cells: Basic Units of Life

Cells are considered to be the basic units of life itself. All living things are made up of cells. A tree is made up of cells, as is an alligator. Some living things only have one cell, such as bacteria. Other living things, such as humans, have trillions of cells in their bodies.

It wasn't until the early 1600s that the existence of cells was discovered. An English scientist, Robert Hooke, built an early microscope. He placed a thin slice of a piece of cork under the microscope, magnified it, and made observations. Imagine his surprise when he saw many small squares in the cork. Robert Hooke thought the small squares resembled the tiny rooms in which monks lived. Robert Hooke named his discovery after these rooms, which were called cells.

As microscopes improved, scientists made important discoveries about cells. They observed that there are many kinds of cells and that these cells are very complicated. Scientists discovered that all cells do not look alike. Many cells apparently specialize in performing a certain kind of function. These cells have shapes that help them do their jobs. For example, muscle cells are elongated. These cells have the ability to expand and contract. Narrow white blood cells have a rounded shape. Their shape assists them in better flowing through veins. Cells that make up the eye are sensitive to light, as is the eye itself.

Microscopes have greatly improved, so much so that Robert Hooke would not believe his eyes if he looked through one today. Scientists' knowledge of cells and their functions have advanced considerably as well. Scientists are continually studying and discovering more each day about cells. One important area of research on cells is how to stop dangerous cells, such as cancer cells, from growing. What started with Robert Hooke and a slice of cork is ongoing, with the health and well-being of humankind as the ultimate goal.

Total Words Read _____
− Errors _____
= CWPM _____

Practice Passage 610

Salmon: Uphill Fighters

0   The salmon is the state fish of Alaska. Named after Greek words
12 meaning "hook" and "nose," salmon are sometimes called the Greek gods of
24 the sea. Salmon contain Omega 3, considered by some to be a miracle
37 ingredient. Omega 3 reportedly helps to reduce the risk of heart attack. Many
50 people consider salmon to be a delicious tasting fish as well. It is a popular
65 choice on many restaurant menus, in grocery stores, and in fish markets.
77 Consequently, commercial fishermen catch millions of salmon each year.

86   As part of their natural life cycle, wild salmon have but one purpose in
100 life. Their only goal is to spawn, or reproduce. Once a salmon has spawned,
114 it dies. Salmon are on the move from the time they are born. Most wild
129 salmon are born in gravel beds in streams or lakes. Recently hatched
141 salmon, called fry, travel far and wide on a quest to find salt water. As they
157 travel, salmon must dodge bigger fish to avoid being eaten. After a period of
171 one to seven years of adventure, a salmon's natural instinct tells it that it is
186 time to return home. Salmon will bravely fight many obstacles as they
198 embark on their trip. Frequently, they battle water currents, swimming
208 upstream to reach the spawning beds where they were born. They then lay
221 and fertilize their eggs. Once that job is completed, the salmon dies. This
234 journey back to their birthplace for the purpose of reproduction is called the
247 salmon run.
249

Total Words Read _____

− Errors _____

= CWPM _____

The Constitution: America's Most Important Document

0	The Constitution is an official plan. It is very important. The
11	Constitution tells how our country should be run. This important plan was
23	written in 1787. The first meeting, or convention, was held on May 25.
36	James Madison was a leader at the convention. He was in favor of a strong
51	national government. He worked very hard and took detailed notes. James
62	Madison is known as the father of the Constitution.
71	Delegates from the 13 states attended the convention. They tried to
82	decide how to elect members of Congress. Some delegates liked the Virginia
94	Plan. This plan said that states with more people should have more
106	members in Congress. Other delegates liked the New Jersey plan. This plan
118	said that all states should have the same number of members in Congress.
131	The delegates decided to compromise. They came up with a plan that
143	created two law-making groups. These law-making groups were called
154	houses. One house would elect delegates based on how many people lived
166	in each state. The other house would elect two delegates from each state
179	regardless of the size of the state. On September 17, 1787, thirty-nine of the
194	fifty-five delegates signed the Constitution. Later, changes were made to the
206	Constitution. These changes are called amendments to the Constitution. The
216	first ten amendments to the Constitution are called the Bill of Rights. In
229	1791, the Bill of Rights was added to the Constitution. Over the next 215
243	years, other changes were made to the Constitution. Our current
253	Constitution has 27 amendments.
257	

Total Words Read _____

− Errors _____

= CWPM _____

Leonardo da Vinci

Leonardo da Vinci was a famous painter. He lived a long time ago during the Italian Renaissance. This was a period of time between 1300 and 1500. Wealthy people and church leaders hired artists. They wanted the artists to paint pictures and make statutes. Da Vinci was one of the greatest artists of the Italian Renaissance.

Leonardo da Vinci painted two very famous paintings. One is called the *Mona Lisa*. The *Mona Lisa* is a picture of a woman. She has a mysterious smile. People wonder why she is smiling and what she is thinking. The other painting is called *The Last Supper*. This painting is a picture of Jesus Christ and his 12 disciples. Da Vinci painted it on a church wall in Italy. These two paintings by Leonardo da Vinci are probably two of the most famous in the entire world.

Although famous as a painter, Da Vinci was also a scientist and an inventor. He studied the human body and how it worked. Da Vinci then made detailed drawings showing how muscles are attached to bones. Da Vinci was fascinated by machines and how they work. Da Vinci invented many machines. For example, he made a flying machine out of wood, cloth, and feathers. It had wings that flapped like a bird. Da Vinci also is credited with inventing military weapons. Leonardo da Vinci was truly a man of many talents.

Practice Passage 613

All That Glitters Might Be Gold

Gold is a valuable metal. For thousands of years, it has been valued for its beautiful yellow color. It also has been valued for its shine and glitter.

Gold can be melted and molded into many different shapes. Gold is used to make beautiful jewelry, coins for various countries, crosses and statues for churches, and, in some cultures, teeth. Gold has been found in many countries all over the world. The Egyptians filled the pharaohs' pyramids with it. The Incas of Peru and the Aztecs of Mexico were experts in using the gold they mined for jewelry and religious statues.

In 1848, gold was found at Sutter's Mill in California. Heavy bars of gold were sent by stagecoach and steamship from California. When people in other parts of the United States saw this gold, they rushed to California, hoping to get rich. These people were called the "forty-niners" because that was the year they started to arrive in California. Gold was found in rushing rivers by prospectors panning for it. Sluice boxes were built on the banks of rivers. The prospectors shoveled the river rock and sand into the sluice box. Water was poured through the sluice box. Gold, which is very heavy, sunk to the bottom of the box while the lighter river rock and sand washed out. Gold has also been found deep in mines. Prospectors found valuable veins of gold in quartz rock deep in the earth and mined the quartz. The quartz rock was crushed and the gold removed from it.

The quest of gold has been the cause of both positive and negative events. The search for this valuable metal caused wars, murders, and whole civilizations to be wiped out. On the other hand, the search for gold led explorers to discover and settle new lands and allowed for the creation of beautiful works of art.

Total Words Read _____
− Errors _____
= CWPM _____

Zeus: Father of the Greek Gods

Gods were important in the ancient Greek religion. The Greeks believed that their gods lived in families and that each god or goddess had a certain kind of power. They also thought that each of the gods had a distinct personality. Sacred places called sanctuaries were built by the Greeks to honor their gods. Greeks prayed to different gods for different reasons. They also made sacrifices to the gods as a way to please them.

Zeus, the god of the sky and of the weather, was also considered the father of all the Greek gods. The Greeks believed that Zeus was the absolute master of all the Greeks, other gods, and perhaps the universe. The Olympic games were actually created to honor Zeus. The games were named after the highest mountain in Greece, Mount Olympus. Ancient Greeks pictured Zeus sitting in a golden throne on top of Mount Olympus. The Greeks believed that Zeus would take pleasure from watching athletes compete in the Olympic games. All Greeks, regardless of where they lived, worshiped Zeus and the other gods in his family. Zeus's wife, Hera, was known as the goddess of marriage. His brother, Poseidon, was the god of the sea. Zeus himself was thought to control the weather. In the Greek people's minds, thunder and lighting occurred as a punishment when Zeus was very angry. One of Zeus's sons, Apollo, was the god of light and health. It was believed that Apollo was responsible for the sun rising and setting each day. The ancient Greeks explained many of the wonders of nature by attributing them to the behavior and personalities of the Greek gods.

King Salmon and Friends

If you are a fish eater, chances are good that you have eaten salmon. Salmon are a popular and plentiful fish. In Alaska alone, more than 173 million salmon were commercially harvested last year.

King salmon are the largest and best-known type of salmon. King salmon average between 20 and 40 pounds but can grow to be much larger. In 1949, a king salmon weighing 126 pounds was caught in a fish trap near Petersburg, Alaska. Ranging from California's Monterey Bay to the Chukchi Sea near Russia, king salmon spend one to seven years in the ocean. Then they, like all salmon, head for their freshwater homes to reproduce or spawn. Once that job is completed, the salmon die. Thus, the natural life cycle of the salmon comes to an end.

In addition to the king salmon, there are four other types of salmon. The coho or silver salmon weighs 8 to 12 pounds on average. The coho is an active salmon—leaping and jumping out of the water when hooked by a fisherman. The sockeye salmon is small, weighing only 4 to 8 pounds. The sockeye is sleek and silver-looking when in the ocean. Once it returns home to spawn, the sockeye salmon turns red. Humpback salmon are the smallest of the Pacific salmon, weighing on average 3 to 4 pounds. The males develop their humpbacks when spawning. They also change color—turning brown to black. The females turn an olive green color. The fifth type of salmon is the chum. These salmon range from the Sacramento River in California to the Mackenzie River in Canada. Chums are the preferred choice of the Alaskan sled dog. Many stores in Alaska sell smoked chum salmon in dog treat packages!

Practice Passage 616

Alexander Graham Bell: Telephone Inventor

0	Alexander Graham Bell invented the telephone in 1876. Bell's father
10	was a teacher of people who were deaf. Alexander became interested in
22	speech and hearing problems. He grew up to become a teacher of the deaf
36	like his father. One of his students later became his wife.
47	Alexander wanted to make speech visible for the deaf. He tried to find
60	a way to record sound vibrations. He worked with another inventor named
72	Thomas Watson. They tried different ways of sending messages. By
82	accident, they found a way to have sound carried by electrical current. After
95	that, it was only a matter of time before they found a way to transmit
110	human sound along a wire.
115	Bell went to the Centennial Exposition of 1876 in Philadelphia. He
126	presented his invention to the public. It was very well received. People
138	could now talk to one another across great distances. Bell continued to
150	improve the telephone. Telephone service companies were organized in
159	England and in the United States. Bell became wealthy and famous. But he
172	never forgot about helping the deaf. If it had not been for Bell's interest in
187	deafness, the telephone would not have been invented. Bell used his own
199	money to set up a fund to study deafness. He was in favor of teaching deaf
215	people to use language instead of signs. Bell was opposed to keeping people
228	who were deaf separate. Many of his methods were used in schools for
241	people who were deaf. Alexander Graham Bell is well-known as the inventor
254	of the telephone. However, he was also an advocate for people who are deaf.
268	

Total Words Read _____

− Errors _____

= CWPM _____

The Thermometer: A Measure of Many Things

Is it cold or hot outside today? We often rely on a thermometer to let us know the temperature. Temperature is a measure of how hot or cold something is. Many factors influence the outside temperature. At certain times of the year, the sun is closer to our part of the earth. During these times, the sun warms the earth, and the temperature is higher. At other times of the year, our part of the earth is tilted away from the sun. Then the temperature is colder. Cloud cover can also influence temperature. If there are few clouds, the temperature is higher. Being close to water is another factor. The air near the water is cooler than inland air. Air high up in the mountains is cooler than desert air. Winds affect temperature as well. When strong winds blow, they usually help cool the air. However, if there is a strong wind blowing in from the hot desert, it will warm up the air.

Meteorologists are people who study the weather. They use thermometers to measure the outside air. But there are other kinds of thermometers as well. Thermometers are also used to determine a person's body temperature. Human beings have a normal body temperature of 98.6 degrees Fahrenheit. Variations from this body temperature can mean that a person is ill. Chemists may use thermometers to check the temperature of a scientific solution. The temperature of the solution can make a difference in a scientist's research findings. Chefs and bakers use thermometers in their work. Meat thermometers indicate whether food is cooked well enough to eat. Candy thermometers are used to help pastry chefs create perfect sweets. Thermometers measure many kinds of things!

Total Words Read _____
− Errors _____
= CWPM _____

Balance of Power: Three Branches of Government

The makers of the United States Constitution did not want to give too much power to one group. They were afraid that it would be dangerous for the country. The lawmakers decided to divide the jobs of the government. They created three branches of government. Article I of the Constitution created the first branch. The first branch is the Legislative Branch. The legislative branch is the Congress. Congress makes the laws of the nation. It also handles money. Congress is responsible for making the money, borrowing money, and collecting taxes. It is also in charge of the military.

The second branch was created as Article II of the Constitution. It is the Executive Branch. The Executive Branch is the President of the United States. The president is responsible for making sure laws are carried out. He is able to put laws into effect by signing them. He can also veto laws he does not like. The president is the commander-in-chief of the nation's armed forces. He appoints people to important positions and makes treaties with other countries.

Article III of the Constitution created the third branch of the government. This third branch is the Judicial Branch. The Judicial Branch is the Supreme Court and other national courts. The Judicial Branch is responsible for explaining what laws mean. This branch decides if current laws passed by Congress follow the intention of the Constitution.

Total Words Read _____
− Errors _____
= CWPM _____

Practice Passage 619

Sequoya: Inventor of the Cherokee Alphabet

0   Sequoya was born in Loudon Country, Tennessee, in about 1760. He
11 was a member of the Cherokee tribe. As a young man, Sequoya became a
25 silversmith. His job was to make objects and jewelry from silver. Sequoya
37 traded his jewelry with the new settlers who had come to his land. Sequoya
51 had never learned how to read. He became interested in how the settlers
64 used marks on paper to record what they said. The Cherokees called these
77 marks "talking leaves." It became apparent to Sequoya that being able to
89 read and write was important. He realized that the Cherokees had no way to
103 do this. As a result, he decided to create a Cherokee alphabet.
115   Sequoya worked for more than 10 years. He matched 85 Cherokee
126 syllables to a written symbol. Finally, the Cherokee alphabet was finished.
137 Sequoya's alphabet was easy to learn. Using this system, most Cherokees
148 learned to read and write in one week's time! Soon thousands of Cherokees
161 were literate. They were able to read the articles Sequoya wrote about their
174 history. The Cherokees made written laws. They also developed a
184 constitution. In the 1827, the Cherokee nation was formed. They adopted
195 English as their second language. Their first newspaper was published in
206 1828. It was called the Cherokee Phoenix. Without Sequoya's invention,
216 none of this would have been possible. Sequoya is honored in California's
228 Sequoia National Park. The giant redwood trees are named after him.
239

Total Words Read _____
- Errors _____
= CWPM _____

Practice Passage 620

George Washington: America's First President

0	George Washington was born in Virginia on February 22, 1732. At that
12	time, Virginia was a colony of England. When George grew up, he joined the
26	Virginia army. He was a good soldier. Soon he became the leader of the
40	army. There were problems in the colonies. Many of the people did not
53	want to belong to England anymore. They felt that the king of England did
67	not treat them fairly. The king made the colonists pay unfair taxes. The king
81	did not want to give the colonies their freedom. So they went to war. This
96	war was called the Revolutionary War. It was also called the War for
109	Independence. George Washington was the leader of the American army in
120	this war. He was a good leader and helped America to win the war.
134	After the war, the colonies became a new country. This country was
146	the United States of America. Americans wanted George Washington to be
157	the leader of the country. He was elected to be the first president in 1789.
172	George Washington was one of the best-loved presidents in American
183	history. He is celebrated in many ways. For example, our nation's capital,
195	Washington, D.C., was named after George Washington. The famous
204	Washington Monument was built to honor George Washington. This tall,
214	pointed building is more than 555 feet high. People can go to the top of the
230	monument. They are able to look over the entire city of Washington, D.C.
243	George Washington's face is on our quarters and dollar bills. George
254	Washington's birthday is celebrated as a national holiday.
262	

Total Words Read _____

− Errors _____

= CWPM _____

Level 6 Practice Passages

Level 7 Practice Passages

701	Polar Exploration
702	Ancient Egyptians Traveled to the New World
703	Alligators: Prehistoric Reptiles
704	Mummy-Making: A Grisly Task
705	Tongass National Forest: America's Rainforest
706	Is It Getting Hotter Out There?
707	Ben Franklin: Author, Inventor, and Statesman
708	George Washington Carver
709	King Tutankhamen's Tomb: A True Treasure Chest
710	The Midwest: America's Breadbasket
711	Put It in Writing
712	King Tutankhamen: An Ancient Murder Mystery?
713	Kwanzaa: A Seven-Day Celebration
714	The United States: Northeast and Southern Regions
715	The River Nile: Ancient Egypt's Gift of Life
716	Julius Caesar: Roman Extraordinaire
717	Getting There from Here
718	Do Paleontologists Carry Pails?
719	Measuring the Weather
720	Rags to Riches: The Horatio Alger Story

Polar Exploration

The polar regions at both ends of the earth have attracted many explorers. Some were scientists. Some were mapmakers. Others went to seek fame as the first explorers to reach the poles. The first polar explorer was a Greek who sailed north around 400 B.C. He probably discovered either Norway or Iceland. No one sailed north for another 1,000 years. Then, Ottar of Norway sailed north from Norway and discovered the White Sea. The Vikings settled both Iceland and Greenland around A.D. 900 However, they did not go any farther north.

Spain and Portugal controlled the southern spice routes to India in the 1500s. The English and the Dutch then tried to find northern routes to India. In 1588, England defeated Spain. England then opened the spice routes to all nations. That made polar exploration no longer necessary. No one ventured south to Antarctica until the 1700s. The English explorer Captain Cook sailed in the area for three years. The Russians sailed east and claimed Alaska in 1728.

Scientists started the next explorations in the 1850s. Geologists wanted to know about the earth's make up. They were interested in the polar regions. Geographers wanted to find the true magnetic North and South Poles. An American, Robert Peary, reached the North Pole on April 6, 1909. A Norwegian, Roald Amundsen, was the first to reach the South Pole on December 14, 1911. Admiral Richard Byrd, an American, was the first to fly over the North Pole. He did so on May 9, 1926. Byrd then turned his attention toward the South Pole. He set up a base camp called "Little America" in Antarctica. Byrd flew over the South Pole on November 29, 1929. The base camp Admiral Byrd set up still serves as a base camp today. It is used for modern scientific exploration by all nations of the world.

Ancient Egyptians Traveled to the New World

　　　　The ancient Egyptians believed that once they died, they would go to a place called the New World. This New World was thought to be a wonderful place where people could live forever. Arriving in the New World was so important to the Egyptian people that they made great plans for this afterlife journey. One important plan was to build pyramids to be used as tombs. Another important plan was to preserve the body. The Egyptians believed that if the dead body decayed, the person's spirit would die and be unable to reach the New World. They developed a process called embalming. This process turned dead bodies into mummies. Usually only the wealthy Egyptians were able to have their bodies turned into mummies.

　　　　The Egyptians believed that travel to the New World was difficult. They thought that the dead needed to have food and drink to make the journey to the New World. Items such as fruit baskets, wine, roasted meat, and bread were placed in the tomb along with the mummy. Sometimes little statues of servants were left in the tombs. The Egyptians believed that a spell would make these servants come to life so that they could work for the dead person in the New World. Many other objects that would be useful in the New World were also placed in tombs. These objects included games, clothes, tools, and jewelry. The Egyptians believed that the afterlife would be similar to current life, so they wanted to be certain that they would have whatever they needed when they arrived in the New World.

Practice Passage 703

Alligators: Prehistoric Reptiles

0	Alligators have lived in the southeastern United States for many
10	centuries. Scientists have studied fossil records of alligators. These records
20	suggest that alligators have lived on earth for 150 million years! That means
33	they were alive when dinosaurs roamed the earth.
41	Native Americans and pioneers occasionally hunted alligators for food.
50	It wasn't until hundreds of years later that alligators were hunted for their
63	skin. Fashion markets started using alligator skin for fine leather products.
74	Beginning in the 1940s, laws were passed to protect alligators. Today,
85	alligators are a protected species.
90	Alligators look like large lizards. They have flat tails and long snouts.
102	Their snouts have nostrils at the end. This allows alligators to breathe while
115	most of their body is underwater. Alligators have four short legs and scaly
128	skin. They can swim very fast by using their long, powerful tails to propel
142	them through the water. Alligators range in size from eight to eleven feet
155	long. The female alligator lays eggs in early spring. She lays about 30 eggs.
169	The eggs are buried in a nest of twigs, sticks, and mud. The nests are built
185	near the water. After she lays the eggs, the mother alligator leaves them
198	alone. The eggs hatch by themselves, and the baby alligators must make
210	their own way to the water. Many baby alligators are eaten by other
223	alligators and creatures on their way to the water. Once the baby alligators
236	are in the water, they are a little safer than they were on the land.
251	Alligators may look cute. However, they are natural predators. Due to
262	their aggressive nature and large size, they can easily kill pets and even
275	humans.
276	

Total Words Read _____

− Errors _____

= CWPM _____

Practice Passage 704

Mummy-Making: A Grisly Task

There were many steps involved in the Egyptian mummification process. First, the dead person's body was washed and placed on a table-like structure. Using an iron hook, the brain was removed by pulling it through the nostrils. Egyptians did not think the brain had much value, so it was discarded. The next step involved removing most of the internal organs such as the stomach, liver, lungs, and intestines with razor-sharp flint knives. The organs were then placed in separate canopic jars. Since the Egyptians believed that the heart was the center of a person's soul, the heart was the only organ left inside the body. The dead body was then placed in a bath of natron, a type of salt, and left to dry for 40 days.

When the drying process was completed, the body was removed from the bath and stuffed with cloth, sand, or sawdust. Many kinds of oil and gum were rubbed into the dry skin of the body. The body was then wrapped in several hundred square yards of linen. The linen cloth used for mummification was old household linen that had been saved for this purpose. Lucky charms, or amulets, were placed between the layers. Egyptians believed that amulets helped to protect the wearer from evil. Elaborate hand-painted masks were placed over the face, head, and shoulders of the body. The mummy was then returned to its family, where it was placed in a human-shaped, wooden coffin. These coffins were often painted to look like portraits of the deceased. Finally, the mummy was placed in the burial room of the pyramid, and the tomb was sealed.

Total Words Read _____
− Errors _____
= CWPM _____

Tongass National Forest: America's Rainforest

0	The Tongass National Forest is in southeast Alaska. It is the second-
12	largest rainforest in the world. Only the Amazon is bigger. The Amazon is a
26	tropical rainforest. Tropical rainforests are found in warm, steamy climates.
36	The Tongass, however, is a temperate rainforest. Temperate rainforests are
46	found in cooler climates.
50	The Tongass is also the largest national forest in the United States. It is
64	about the size of New Jersey. The Tongass covers 17 million acres of land.
78	Five thousand miles of the Tongass are along the southeastern Alaskan
89	shoreline. Visitors to the Tongass can see ice fields, glaciers, and four snow-
102	capped mountain ranges. There are also hundreds of islands covered with
113	dense forests. Hemlock and cedar are the most common trees found in the
126	Tongass Islands. Caves, rivers, and lakes lie within the Tongass National
137	Forest. The woods are home to many types of wildlife. These include brown
150	and black bears, wolves, moose, goats, and porcupines. The Tongass has
161	one of the world's largest concentrations of bald eagles.
170	The Tongass serves many functions. It is a wilderness preservation
180	and recreation area. There are 13 campgrounds and 150 recreational cabins.
191	Nineteen wilderness areas and 450 miles of hiking trails attract many
202	visitors each year. The Tongass is also used for mining and timber
214	harvesting. The Tongass provided the timber needed for both World War I
226	and World War II. Only three percent of the Tongass has been harvested in
240	the last 94 years. That means that the forest consists of 97 percent old
254	growth—trees that have been left undisturbed.
261	

Total Words Read _____
− Errors _____
= CWPM _____

Practice Passage 706

Is It Getting Hotter Out There?

0	There is a lot of talk about the earth getting warmer and warmer.
13	Scientists have done a great deal of research on global warming. They have
26	investigated claims that the earth is warming up each year. They have also
39	researched claims that all of the ice at the Poles is melting. Some scientists
53	believe that aerosols, which propel spray material, are eating the ozone
64	layer. Without the protection of the ozone layer, certain harmful rays and
76	radiation from the sun could make their way to the earth's surface. Those
89	rays and radiation could cause cancer.
95	Some other scientists believe that the upsurge in the earth's
105	temperature is just due to the natural fluctuation in the earth's temperature.
117	There is agreement among scientists that the temperature of the earth has
129	risen almost two degrees in the last 150 years. However, the cause of the
143	temperature rise is still being studied and debated. Some scientists have
154	predicted that temperatures will again rise in the next one hundred years. If
167	that is the case, some of the ice at the Poles will melt. If that melt occurs,
184	the water levels around the entire earth will rise almost twenty inches.
196	Floods will occur all around the globe.
203	Scientists continue to study the causes and effects of global warming.
214	So far, they have not reached agreement on its causes or its solution. Laws
228	have been passed to ban some types of chemicals known to be dangerous to
242	the environment. Scientists are studying other chemicals that are suspected
252	of damaging the ozone layer. The outcome of their studies will probably
264	result in more laws regarding chemicals in our atmosphere. Global warming
275	is a serious topic. It is a threat to our environment. We should continue to
290	be aware of it and study its effects.
298	

Total Words Read _____

− Errors _____

= CWPM _____

Ben Franklin: Author, Inventor, and Statesman

0	Benjamin Franklin is a famous name in American history. He was born
12	in Boston, Massachusetts, on January 17, 1706. There were 17 children in
24	Ben's family. When Ben was only 12 years old, he went to work in a
39	printing shop and learned to use a printing press. In 1723, Ben moved to
53	Philadelphia at the age of 17. He quickly found a job as a printer and settled
69	down in his new city. Ben Franklin wrote and published a book called *Poor*
83	*Richard's Almanac.* This book included a calendar and information about
93	the weather, the sun, and the moon. It also gave practical advice. Ben
106	Franklin is the author of famous sayings, such as "A penny saved is a penny
121	earned" and "Early to bed, early to rise makes a man healthy, wealthy, and
135	wise," which were published in the *Almanac.*
142	In addition to being an author, Benjamin Franklin was also an
153	inventor. He invented the Franklin stove, for example. The Franklin stove
164	used less wood to produce more heat than a fireplace. He also invented
177	lightning rods. These rods conducted lightning into the ground. This helped
188	to prevent lightning from striking buildings and causing fires. Franklin is
199	credited with starting the first lending library in America. He also developed
211	bifocal glasses. Bifocals enable people to see close up and at a distance
224	using the same glasses.
228	Franklin loved Philadelphia. He worked hard to help his new country.
239	In 1766, Franklin went to England on the colonies' behalf. He argued against
252	the Stamp Act. The Stamp Act made the colonists pay unfair taxes. Benjamin
265	Franklin persuaded France to help the colonies. Many people give Benjamin
276	Franklin credit for helping the colonies win the American Revolution.
286	

Total Words Read _____

− Errors _____

= CWPM _____

George Washington Carver

George Washington Carver was born a slave in Missouri in 1864. As a child, Carver was interested in plants. He dreamed of going to college to study farming. Carver worked many jobs in order to earn money for his education. He grew up to be a famous American chemist.

After he graduated from college, Carver became a teacher at Tuskegee Institute. Carver wanted to help the farmers who lived in the southern United States. Their farmland was worn out from only growing one kind of crop: cotton. Carver talked the farmers into growing other crops, such as peanuts and sweet potatoes. Carver was also interested in scientific research. He spent a lot of time studying peanuts and sweet potatoes. By experimenting in his lab, Carver was able to discover more than 300 ways to use peanuts. Many people think he was responsible for inventing peanut butter. Other products that he made from peanuts were soap, shampoo, ink, cooking oil, and cheese. From the sweet potato, Carver made starch, vinegar, ginger, and instant coffee.

George Washington Carver received many awards for his research findings. Money was not important to George Washington Carver. He never accepted a raise and sometimes did not even cash his paycheck. Carver also never applied for a patent on his inventions. He believed that God was responsible for his inventions. So he did not think he should claim them as his own. Carver was a quiet man who did not like crowds. He was most happy when in his laboratory doing research to help farmers. He donated most of the money he earned to Tuskegee Institute for future scientific studies.

Practice Passage 709

King Tutankhamen's Tomb: A True Treasure Chest

0	King Tut is probably the best known of the Egyptian pharaohs. He is
13	famous simply for the discovery of his tomb. Following his death more than
26	3,000 years ago, King Tut's mummy and tomb were laid to rest in Egypt's
40	Valley of the Kings. This valley was the burial ground for many of the New
55	Kingdom pharaohs. King Tut's tomb remained sealed and buried until its
66	discovery on November 22, 1922.
71	The tomb was discovered by an archaeologist named Howard Carter. A
82	rich man named Lord Carnarvon hired Howard Carter. Lord Carnarvon had
93	bought the right to dig in the Valley of the Kings. He and Howard Carter had
109	been looking for the tomb for five years. Finally, they found steps leading to
123	the entrance to the tomb. The tomb itself consisted of four small rooms,
136	each filled with golden treasure. It was obvious that ancient tomb robbers
148	had broken into the first room in King Tut's tomb. However, over 600 items
162	and the burial room had been left untouched. The tomb was filled with
175	beautiful objects made of gold, precious stones, and detailed carvings. The
186	most exciting find was the burial chamber containing King Tut's mummy.
197	The mummy was buried in a solid gold coffin. Its head and shoulders were
211	covered with a beautiful golden mask depicting the face of King Tut. The
224	discovery of King Tut's tomb was an exciting and important find because it
237	was the only tomb of an ancient Egyptian king to be found almost
250	completely intact. Every item in the tomb was photographed, measured, and
261	recorded before it was taken away. It took archaeologists many years to
273	completely clear the tomb. King Tut's treasures are on display in the
285	Museum of Cairo.
288	

Total Words Read _____

− Errors _____

= CWPM _____

The Midwest: America's Breadbasket

0	The Midwestern region of the continental United States consists of ten
11	states. These states are located in the middle section of the country. They
24	touch all of the other United States regions, as well as Canada. The
37	Midwestern region also includes the Great Lakes. The Great Lakes contain
48	almost all of the fresh water in the United States. North Dakota, South
61	Dakota, Nebraska, and Kansas are among the Midwestern states. So are
72	Minnesota, Iowa, Missouri, and Wisconsin. The other states in this region
83	are Wisconsin, Illinois, Michigan, Indiana, and Ohio. The Midwestern states
93	first belonged to France. The United States bought these states from France
105	in 1803.
107	Most of the land in the Midwest is widespread prairie land. The land is
121	very good for farming. In fact, the Midwest is known as the breadbasket of
135	the United States. Most of the nation's wheat and corn is grown in the
149	Midwest. Kansas is the top producer of wheat. Valuable minerals can be
161	found in the Midwest as well. Consequently, there are a number of iron and
175	steel factories in Midwestern cities such as Detroit, Michigan. There are
186	some famous landmarks in the Midwest. Chicago, Illinois, is the largest city
198	in the Midwestern region. Chicago is home to the Sears Tower, the tallest
211	building in North America. The Black Hills of South Dakota are home to Mt.
225	Rushmore. Carved into the side of Mt. Rushmore are the heads of four
238	legendary United States presidents. They include George Washington,
246	Thomas Jefferson, Theodore Roosevelt, and Abraham Lincoln.
253	

Total Words Read _____

− Errors _____

= CWPM _____

Practice Passage 71

Put It in Writing

When you do your homework or write a letter to a friend, the marks you make on the paper stand for the sounds you make when you talk. Writing is a way of turning sounds into marks that fit together and make words. With writing, people can "talk" to one another from miles and miles away. Writing is a marvelous invention that began many thousands of years ago.

Historians believe that writing began in ancient Mesopotamia. Ancient people called Sumerians invented writing. Writing was probably invented out of economic necessity. People needed a way to keep track of products that they sold or bought from one another. The first written symbols were pictographs. Pictographs are pictures that stand for ideas. Sumerians drew pictographs on damp clay using a thin plant stalk. By about 2500 B.C., Sumerians were using a type of writing called cuneiform. They had taken picture symbols and made them wedge-shaped. Cuneiform had about 600 symbols. Some symbols were made up of only one wedge. Other symbols were more complicated. These could have up to 30 wedges. This system of writing was used in the Middle East for almost 2,000 years. Over the years, archaeologists have found many clay tablets with cuneiform symbols.

Eventually another group of ancient people invented a different type of writing. The Phoenicians used a system with only twenty-two symbols. Each of these symbols represented one sound. This system became the first alphabet. Just as there are different languages all over the world, there are different kinds of writing. Arabic writing looks like flowing curves, with dots and dashes mixed in. Chinese writing looks like little squares, windows, and stick figures. Whatever kind of writing it may be, the marks stand for a people's spoken language.

Total Words Read _____
− Errors _____
= CWPM _____

Practice Passage 712

King Tutankhamen: An Ancient Murder Mystery?

Although King Tut has been dead for more than 3,000 years, historians are still debating about how he died. King Tut was born in southern Egypt around 1330 B.C. He became king at nine years of age. The previous ruler of Egypt was King Akhenaton. He had tried to make the Egyptians worship Amon, the sun god, rather than the more traditional gods. When King Akhenaton died, the Egyptian people who wanted to restore Egypt's old religion placed King Tut on the throne. They wanted to make King Tut seem older and more capable of ruling the country. So they married him to the previous king's wife. King Tut did not actually govern the kingdom. His uncle and advisors took care of that job. King Tut's reign was an unimportant one.

King Tut became famous in 1922 when his tomb was discovered by a British archaeologist named Howard Carter. King Tut's tomb was the only Egyptian tomb in history found with most of its treasures intact. Scientists discovered that King Tut's mummy had a lump on the back of the head. That led scientists to speculate that King Tut may have died of a brain tumor. Recently, however, new X-ray analysis indicated that King Tut may have been murdered in his sleep. The injury, a trauma specialist believes, is consistent with a blow from behind. The suggestion that King Tut may have been murdered leads historians to the controversial questions: Who killed King Tut and why?

Total Words Read _____
− Errors _____
= CWPM _____

Level 7 Practice Passages

Practice Passage 713

Kwanzaa: A Seven-Day Celebration

0   Many African American people celebrate Kwanzaa. It was reported in
10 *The New York Times* that more than 18 million people worldwide celebrate
22 this holiday. Kwanzaa comes from Swahili, an African language. The word
33 "kwanzaa" means "first fruit of the harvest." During Kwanzaa, people
43 celebrate by getting together with family and friends. Kwanzaa begins the
54 day after Christmas. It lasts until New Year's Day.
63   Kwanzaa is neither a religious nor a political holiday. It is based on
76 seven guiding principles. The principles focus on African values. For
86 example, one guiding principle is the importance of family togetherness.
96 Another is self-determination. Collective work and responsibility are guiding
106 principles. So is cooperative economics. The other principles are purpose,
116 creativity, and faith.
119   For each of the seven nights of Kwanzaa, people celebrate and share
131 food. They eat chicken, yams, vegetables, rice, and beans. During Kwanzaa
142 celebrations, candles are lit. A candleholder called a kinara is used. The
154 kinara holds seven candles. A straw mat is often used during Kwanzaa
166 celebrations. Symbols of Kwanzaa are placed upon this straw mat. For
177 example, one of the symbols of Kwanzaa is an ear of corn. It is the symbol
193 for a child. Many families place one ear of corn for each child on the straw
209 mat. The colors of Kwanzaa are black, red, and green. These colors are used
223 for decorating the home with balloons, flowers, and prints. Gifts are usually
235 exchanged on the last day of Kwanzaa. These gifts are often homemade and
248 are educational or artistic. Kwanzaa is truly a special seven-day celebration!
260

Total Words Read _____

− Errors _____

= CWPM _____

Practice Passage 714

The United States: Northeast and Southern Regions

0	The United States of America is a big country. It is made up of 50
15	states and Washington, D.C. The "D.C." means District of Columbia.
25	Washington, D.C. is the capital of the United States. Of the 50 states in the
40	United States, 48 are on the continent of North America. These 48 states
53	touch one another. They are known as the continental United States. The
65	other two states in the United States are Hawaii and Alaska.
76	The continental United States is divided into six regions. The first
87	region is called the Northeastern Region. It consists of nine states. Three of
100	the eight mid Atlantic states are also included in the Northeastern Region.
112	These states are New Jersey, New York, and Pennsylvania. The other six
124	states in the Northeastern Region are also known as the New England states.
137	They include Maine, Massachusetts, New Hampshire, Vermont, Rhode
145	Island, and Connecticut. Captain John Smith called these states New
155	England because they reminded him of England. Many important cities such
166	as New York City, Boston, and Philadelphia are located in the northeast.
178	There are also many famous historical sites.
185	The Southern states are another region in the United States. There are
197	twelve southern states. Virginia, West Virginia, Kentucky, and Tennessee
206	are southern states. So are North Carolina, South Carolina, Georgia, and
217	Florida. Arkansas, Mississippi, Louisiana, and Alabama are remaining
225	southern states. Many of these states have a warm climate and rich, fertile
238	soil. Those conditions were perfect for growing tobacco and cotton. Large
249	plantations, which relied on slave labor, dominated the Southern economy
259	at one time. Conflicts over slavery led to the Civil War in 1861.
272	

Total Words Read _____

− Errors _____

= CWPM _____

Level 7 Practice Passages

The River Nile: Ancient Egypt's Gift of Life

The Nile River is the longest river in the entire world. It flows from the lakes of central Africa, over 4,000 miles, to the Mediterranean Sea. Unlike most rivers, the Nile flows from south to north. If you were to look at the Nile River on a map, it would appear to be flowing upstream!

Egypt is a country surrounded by natural barriers. Parts of the Sahara Desert border Egypt on the east and west. The Mediterranean Sea is Egypt's northern border. Mountains provide a southern border. These natural barriers protected ancient Egypt against invaders. Without the Nile River, though, Egypt would be desert land. Ancient Egyptians depended upon the Nile for water as well as for life itself. The Nile River floods every year. When it floods, it leaves behind rich soil. These soil deposits turn the lands surrounding the Nile into fertile farmland. Consequently, ancient Egyptians were able to develop an agricultural economy. Since the Nile River flooding was predictable, Egyptian farmers were able to practice irrigation farming. All of the rich soil carried by the Nile River was deposited into a triangle-shaped delta at the mouth of the river. The Egyptian people fished the Nile and ate the edible birds, such as ducks and geese, that made their homes in the marshlands. A long, thin grass called papyrus grew along the banks of the Nile River. Ancient Egyptians used papyrus to make many useful items such as sandals, boats, and baskets. They even developed a type of writing paper from papyrus. In fact, our word "paper" was derived from the word "papyrus."

Total Words Read _____

− Errors _____

= CWPM _____

Practice Passage 716

Julius Caesar: Roman Extraordinaire

0   Do you ever wonder how the calendar months got their names? You
12 may be surprised to know that the origins of our modern-day calendar date
26 back to the time of the ancient Romans.

34   Julius Caesar, a famous general in ancient Rome, was responsible for
45 the development of the calendar. Caesar discovered in 46 B.C. that the Roman
58 calendar was three months behind the sun. So he added three months to the
72 Roman calendar. Caesar also rearranged the way in which the calendar was
84 organized. In appreciation for his efforts, the Roman Senate named the
95 month of July after Julius Caesar.

101   Julius Caesar was well known for his military pursuits. Caesar ended
112 the Roman Republic in 46 B.C. when he started a civil war. After three years
127 of fighting, Caesar triumphed. He defeated his Roman rivals and was able to
140 gain control of the country. In 49 B.C., Caesar declared himself dictator, a
153 ruler with absolute power. Caesar was not well liked as a dictator. The
166 Roman people were afraid that Caesar was planning to make himself a king
179 and establish a dynasty. If that were the case, Caesar's family would rule
192 Rome even after his death. The Roman Senate would then have no say in
206 selecting their own leader. Desperate to prevent this, more than 60 senators
218 planned Caesar's assassination. The leader of the plot was Brutus, a man
230 Caesar considered to be a friend. When Caesar was first attacked, he tried to
244 defend himself. When he recognized that his friend Brutus had turned against
256 him, Caesar cried out, saying, "You too, Brutus?" and fell to the ground.
269

Total Words Read _____

− Errors _____

= CWPM _____

Practice Passage 717

Getting There from Here

How do I get there? That is a question that humans have been asking for many lifetimes. Moving from one place to another in prehistoric times was done on foot. People simply walked to get where they were going. When the wheel was invented, moving from one place to another certainly became easier. As more time passed, the wheel was attached to wagons of various sizes. Wagons became handcarts, carriages, stagecoaches, small carts, large covered wagons, and huge freight wagons.

Traveling by water was undertaken when people built floating rafts and boats that carried only one person. As people became more adept at building watercraft, the boats and rafts became much larger and carried more people and supplies. Sails were attached to the watercraft so that people could move much more quickly across the seas. When the steam engine was invented, it was joined with the wheel on land to power locomotives, and on water to power huge paddlewheels. When the gasoline engine was invented, it was used to power cars, trains, ships, and planes. Trains now move from one city to another so quickly that they are called "bullet trains." Supersonic jets fly faster than the speed of sound and can cross oceans in three to four hours. People began to move quite quickly and efficiently over land, water, and the air. With the invention of rockets, it became possible to go into space to explore the moon and the outer reaches of our planetary system. Traveling from one place to another has certainly improved over time.

Total Words Read _____
− Errors _____
= CWPM _____

Practice Passage 718

Do Paleontologists Carry Pails?

What are paleontologists and what do they do? Do they make pails or carry pails with them in their work? Paleontologists do not make pails. However, they may carry one containing a fossil or two.

Paleontologists are scientists. They find fossils and study them. Fossils are the remains of dead plants and animals that lived long, long ago. Fossils are often found in rock that was once soil. Over time, the soil hardened and became rock. Paleontologists look for evidence in the fossils in order to know what the earth was like long ago.

Some of the paleontologist's work is done out in the field where the fossils have been found. Paleontologists may be a part of the dig and actually move the earth themselves. Some paleontologists study the fossils of insects only, or animals, or fish. Others may study the fossils of long-ago plants and leaves. Some paleontologists have specialized in reptiles, such as dinosaurs. After fossils are found in a dig, molds are made of their remains. The fossils are then carefully packed and sent to a laboratory so they may be studied using highly technical scientific equipment. Equipment such as high-tech microscopes and x-ray machines help the scientists in their studies.

It is through the work of the paleontologists that we know about life long ago. Due to their findings, we know what plants and animals looked like in prehistoric times. Paleontologists are responsible for our knowing about the dinosaurs who lived on earth millions of years ago. They also help us to understand how prehistoric animals and fish of long ago evolved into the animals that we know today. Paleontologists, like all scientists, must also be good writers. They must write reports stating what they have learned from their fossil studies. Paleontologists all over the world share information with one another. That shared knowledge helps us to understand not only what the earth was like in prehistoric times, but also how we can protect the earth for the future.

Total Words Read _____

− Errors _____

= CWPM _____

Practice Passage 719

Measuring the Weather

Many scientists study and measure the weather. They do this to give the best information they can about the weather. Scientists who study and forecast the weather are called meteorologists. Meteorologists use many tools in their jobs. Each tool they use gives them some weather information. For example, they use a thermometer to measure the temperature of the air. A barometer tells them the air pressure. A tool called an anemometer helps them to measure the wind's speed. They take all of the information from their different tools. Then they study it.

Based on their studies, meteorologists forecast the weather. Sometimes the weather is exactly as the meteorologists predicted. Other times, the weather is not anything like its forecast. Predicting the weather is a science. It is not a perfect science however. Today meteorologists can predict severe weather patterns and send out warnings. Meteorologists have saved many lives by warning people about severe weather in their areas. Computers and technology help them to know what each day's weather will be. Many people rely on meteorologists and the information they gather to predict the weather. Farmers must know when to plant crops. Truck drivers need to know which routes to drive. Pilots need to know about possible storms in their flight paths. Ordinary people might need to know how to dress on certain days. They may want to know if it will be a good day for outside activities. People are dependent upon meteorologists to provide them with information so that they can make informed decisions about their daily activities.

Total Words Read _____

− Errors _____

= CWPM _____

Rags to Riches: The Horatio Alger Story

Horatio Alger was a popular 19th-century American writer who wrote more than one hundred thirty books for young boys. Alger was raised in a religious home. He graduated from Harvard Divinity School in 1852. Instead of becoming a minister though, Alger became a teacher and a writer. For a time, he even lived the life of a bohemian in Paris. Alger returned to America and became a minister for a short time. Then he became a social worker in New York City. It was through this work that Horatio Alger decided to use the theme of "rags to riches" in his writing. In each of Alger's stories, the main character was always a teenage boy from a poor family. Through hard work, honesty, and determination, the boy was able to overcome many problems. In the end, the boy achieved the American dream. Every book had the same message: Anyone, even a poor, homeless boy, could become successful if he tries his best and always tries to do the right thing.

Alger's most popular books were the *Ragged Dick* series, the *Luck and Pluck* series, and the *Tattered Tom* series. These dime novels, as they were called, were known for their illustrated covers. They were cheap and easily found at newsstands and grocery stores.

During his time, Horatio Alger was one of America's best-selling authors. He was also the greatest salesman of the American dream.

Level 8 Practice Passages

801	Greek Columns: Capital Differences
802	Where in the World Did They Get Their Names?
803	Ben Franklin: Scientist and Inventor
804	Anasazi Apartments
805	Animals: How Do We Tell Them Apart?
806	Ancient Greeks: Ancestors of Today
807	Friendship Bell: An International Symbol
808	Pearl Harbor: Surprise Attack
809	Roman Gladiators: Bloody Entertainers
810	Rocky Mountain States: Nature's Wonderland
811	Archaeology: Digging for Buried Treasure
812	Oak Ridge: Secret City
813	Olympic Torchbearers: Keepers of the Flame
814	The Cherokee Trail of Tears: 1828 to 1839
815	John James Audubon: A Natural Artist
816	Why Seven Wonders?
817	Southwestern United States: The Mighty Four
818	Pacific Coast: The Last Frontier
819	Graphite Reactor: The World's First Nuclear Reactor
820	Olympics: An Ancient Tradition

Greek Columns: Capital Differences

Greek architecture is famous for its use of graceful and beautiful columns. During the classical Greek architecture period, there were three types of columns used in Greek temples. The columns differ because of their tops, which are called capitals. Each of the three Greek capital styles developed in a different part of Greece. The three types of columns are Doric, Ionic, and Corinthian.

The Doric column is the oldest and plainest. It is also the heaviest and the only one without a base. The Doric columns of ancient Greece were influenced by Egyptian architecture. These columns were somewhat squat when compared to the other, more elegant, types of columns. Doric architecture was widely used by the Spartans.

The second type of column is the Ionic. Ionic columns are lighter than the Doric and have two curly scrolls that border the ends at each side of the capital. Ionic columns are more slender than Doric columns and have large bases. They are simple, yet decorative.

The Corinthian columns are similar to the Ionian columns in shape. However, the Corinthian columns are elaborately decorated. They are decorated with carvings of leaf-like structures, which appear to be flowering. The Corinthian columns were not as widely used as the Doric and the Ionic. The Roman Coliseum was built with all three types of Greek columns. The ground floor of the Coliseum is Doric, the first floor is Ionic, and the second and third floors are Corinthian. The influence of Greek architecture can be found in many places all over the world.

Total Words Read _____
− Errors _____
= CWPM _____

Practice Passage 802

Where in the World Did They Get Their Names?

      Places all over the world have unusual names. The stories behind how they got their names are sometimes funny, descriptive, and strange. For example, centuries ago, the owner of Blarney Castle in Ireland talked an enemy out of attacking his castle by using clever words and flattery. People who are clever with words, know how to flatter others, and talk their way out of trouble are said to have kissed the Blarney Stone. Today, tourists come from all over the world to kiss the Blarney Stone and get the gift of gab!

      The Amazon River is another example of an interesting name origin. The Amazon, in South America, is the world's second-longest river. Spanish explorers discovered the river. South American natives, wearing tall headdresses and grass skirts, attacked them. The natives reminded the Spanish of the Greek legend about tall women warriors. These women warriors were called Amazons, so the explorers named the river the Amazon.

      The Pacific Ocean was named by a Spanish explorer named Magellan. Magellan found the ocean to be very peaceful. So he named it the Pacific Ocean after the Spanish word for "peaceful." It is ironic because the Pacific Ocean is probably the stormiest ocean. Magellan must have been lucky enough to sail when the ocean was calm.

Total Words Read _____
− Errors _____
= CWPM _____

Practice Passage 803

Ben Franklin: Scientist and Inventor

Ben Franklin was our country's first scientist and inventor. Ben was born in Boston, Massachusetts, on January 17, 1706. Ben's father immigrated to America from England. His father opened a shop where he made soap and candles. As a young boy, Ben always enjoyed science. He was interested in everything around him. One of Ben's most helpful and practical inventions was his Franklin stove. His stove improved heating in colonial homes. It helped to make the early American homes much more comfortable during the cold winter months. Ben's invention also helped create a huge stove-building industry in America.

Ben was also interested in electricity. He was fascinated by lightning and wondered how it worked. By flying a kite with a metal key attached to it during a thunderstorm, Ben proved that lighting was actually electricity. He also invented the lightning rod, which saved many homes from fire. The lightning rod sends the electrical charge away from the building so it doesn't cause it to catch on fire. When Ben published his book, *Observations in Electricity,* he became famous all over the world.

Ben was instrumental in starting the science of weather prediction. Ben Franklin also studied and invented many other common objects we still use today. Bifocal glasses, corn brooms, and the platform rocker are just some of the many inventions that sprang from Ben's brilliant mind. He helped farmers by showing them how to add lime to their fields to grow better crops. Ben Franklin also helped to write our Declaration of Independence, and served as America's first ambassador to England. He was a very talented man and a great American.

Total Words Read _____
- Errors _____
= CWPM _____

Practice Passage 804

Anasazi Apartments

In 1888, an exciting discovery was made in southwestern Colorado. Two cowboys were crossing a mesa on horseback. They were searching for lost cattle. They came to the edge of a large canyon and gazed over it. The cowboys were amazed to see something that looked like a large city hanging off the cliffs! These two cowboys, Richard Wetherill and Charlie Mason, were the first to discover what appeared to be ancient apartment houses. The houses were made of adobe, clay, sand, and bits of straw. The cowboys called them "Cliff Palace." Scientists came to study Cliff Palace. The scientists discovered that these cliff-like apartment houses were probably built around A.D.1200. The scientists determined that Cliff Palace had 151 rooms with 23 kivas. Kivas are special rooms built underground. The Anasazi tribes most likely built Cliff Palace. "Anasazi" is a Navajo Indian word that means "ancient ones."

Special scientists called archeologists studied the tower-like structures, hoping for clues about the people who lived in them. Archeologists believe that the Anasazi built their cliff dwellings to protect themselves from their enemies. However, it seems that these tribes only lived in the apartment-like structures for 75 to 100 years. By A.D. 1300, the Anasazi had migrated to other places. Scientists have many theories as to why the tribes abandoned their homes. However, they may never know the real reason behind the move.

Today the Cliff Palace is preserved in Mesa Verde National Park. Mesa Verde National Park is the only national park that protects and preserves manmade structures such as these ancient cliff dwellings. Visitors to the park can view over 4,000 historical ruins. These tours can be strenuous though. The cliff dwellings are located at about 7,000 feet in elevation. Tourists must hike 100 feet into a steep canyon. Once inside Cliff Palace, four tall ladders must be climbed. A trip into Cliff Palace is only recommended for people in good physical condition!

Total Words Read _____

− Errors _____

= CWPM _____

Animals: How Do We Tell Them Apart?

There are over one million kinds or species of animals on our earth. With that many species of animals, it was important for scientists to find some way to group the species in order to tell them apart. After studying many different ways, scientists decided to use bones as the first big way to group animals.

If an animal has its bones inside its body, including a backbone, it belongs in the group called vertebrates. If an animal has no bones inside its body and does not have a backbone, it belongs to the group called invertebrates. If you think about bones and whether or not a particular animal has them, you will always know whether an animal is a vertebrate or an invertebrate. For example, the bear, the cow, and the alligator are vertebrates because their bones are inside their bodies. They also have a backbone. On the other hand, the jellyfish, the fly, and the earthworm are all invertebrates because they have no bones inside their bodies and no backbones. There are many more invertebrates than vertebrates on our earth.

After scientists decided on these two main groups for classifying animals, they then made other decisions. They looked at each group separately. They then further divided the two big groups into smaller groups by looking at other differences. For example, one group of vertebrates was called mammals because the mother feeds her babies with milk from her body. If vertebrates have feathers and have wings, they are a group called birds. If vertebrates have dry skin and scales, they belong to the reptile group. But because they all have bones inside their bodies, they all belong to the large group called vertebrates.

Ancient Greeks: Ancestors of Today

What does modern life in the 21st century have in common with the civilization of ancient Greece? You may be surprised to find out just how many similarities exist. The ancient Greek civilization existed between 500 and 323 B.C. This time in history was known as the classical Greek period. Ancient Greek influence is prevalent in our modern times. The Greeks can be credited with the beginning of western civilization. For instance, the ancient Greeks were the founders of democracy as we know it today. In Athens, around 510 B.C., the citizens decided that the people would have a say in how they were governed. The word "democracy" comes from two Greek words that together mean "rule of the people." Many of the government buildings in the United States are modeled after Greek architecture. This probably reflects Greek influence in government as well as in design. Greek architects designed beautiful structures using columns to support the roof.

Greek influence can also be seen in the arts. High school students today read the epic poems *The Odyssey* and *The Iliad,* written by the Greek author Homer. Epic poems are very long poems that describe the brave deeds of heroes. Greek theater is still enjoyed today as well. The Greeks were famous for developing Greek tragedies and Greek comedies. The Greek tragedies are ageless because they deal with human behavior. The Greek comedy, particularly in the form of political satire, is still in vogue.

Greek philosophers were known as great thinkers. They did not accept the common explanation of the time that the Greek gods were responsible for all events. Instead, they searched for answers by questioning. The techniques developed by the famous Greek philosopher Socrates are still used in colleges today.

Friendship Bell: An International Symbol

An international friendship bell stands in the community of Oak Ridge, Tennessee. The friendship bell was the result of a community project. The project was undertaken to celebrate Oak Ridge's 50th birthday. A friendship bell typically is a symbol of universal peace. It also stands for friendship and understanding among all people in the world.

The friendship bell in Oak Ridge is unique for two reasons. First of all, there are thought to be only two such bells in the world. Second, the friendship bell is the first United States and Japanese monument at any Manhattan Project site. The Manhattan Project was in effect from 1942 to 1946. It was responsible for developing the first atomic weapons. The atom bomb was used to bring an end to World War II.

The idea of the international friendship bell was suggested by an Oak Ridge resident who was Japanese American. Her name was Shigeko Uppuluri. The friendship bell is a traditional Japanese bell. In fact, it was cast in solid bronze by a Japanese bellmaker. The bell is nearly five feet in diameter and almost seven feet tall. It weighs 8,250 pounds! Another Oak Ridger, named Susana Harris, designed the bell's two large panels. The top panel is dedicated to Tennessee and the bottom panel to Japan. The panels depict the official plants, birds, and flowers of each respective area. Other parts of the panel list important historical dates from Pearl Harbor through the end of World War II. Most importantly, the friendship bell incorporates a message of international peace.

Practice Passage 808

Pearl Harbor: Surprise Attack

On the early morning of December 7, 1941, most of Pearl Harbor was sleeping. Only a few sailors were on Sunday duty. Seven of the United States fleet's great battleships were floating in the harbor. Another ship was in dry-dock. Eight cruisers, forty-one destroyers, and five submarines were also present. All three of the fleet's aircraft carriers were away from Pearl Harbor on other duties. The United States naval forces were not on any type of alert. The United States had not yet entered World War II.

Quietly in the early morning darkness, the Japanese task force approached the U.S. fleet. At 6 a.m. Hawaiian time, 189 Japanese warplanes were flown off the carrier decks. They headed toward the north point of Oahu at 7:50 a.m. and then separated. Dive-bombers turned toward the airbases where the American planes sat neatly on the ground. Meanwhile, forty torpedo planes, followed by fifty horizontal bombers, attacked the sitting fleet. Behind them came fifty Japanese fighters. These fighters were prepared to stop any American air defense. One hour later came the second wave of Japanese aircraft. Fifty-four horizontal bombers, eighty-one dive-bombers, and thirty-six fighters were ready to reinforce the initial attack and destroy whatever had been missed.

In one hour and forty-five minutes, the Japanese had knocked the heart out of the American fleet. They were successful due to their attack being a total surprise. The attack on Pearl Harbor was enough to give Japan an initial overwhelming advantage. Americans were at first completely shocked and then enraged. Less than 24 hours after the first bomb was dropped, the United States Congress voted to declare war on Japan.

Total Words Read _____
− Errors _____
= CWPM _____

Level 8 Practice Passages

Practice Passage 809

Roman Gladiators: Bloody Entertainers

Perhaps you, like many Americans today, are an avid sports fan. If so, you probably enjoy going to a sports stadium to be entertained. The citizens of ancient Rome also enjoyed sports. In A.D. 106, Romans gathered in large arenas, such as the famous Roman Coliseum. They came to enjoy an afternoon of free food and exciting entertainment. The Romans loved to watch the gladiators! Gladiator fighting began in Rome in 246 B.C. Three brothers organized one of the first gladiator fights. They did this as a way of honoring their dead father. Then, gladiator fighting became a popular event at funerals. Eventually, Roman gladiator fighting became a profit-making sports event.

There are differences between the Roman gladiators and the professional fighters of today. For one thing, Roman gladiators were armed with weapons such as swords. In fact, the word "gladiator" comes from a Latin word meaning "sword." Another difference is that the Roman gladiators fought to the death. Many of the gladiators were slaves who were bought to become gladiators. Other gladiators were criminals or prisoners of war. These gladiators could earn their freedom if they survived for three to five years. Unfortunately, most gladiators did not live that long even though they only fought two or three times a year. Sometimes free men volunteered to become gladiators. Like modern-day athletes, Roman gladiators were often viewed as heroes. This was especially true in times of peace. When Romans did not have war heroes to look up to, they admired their gladiators. The gladiator games were extremely violent. However, the ancient Romans found the games entertaining. Today, the term "Roman holiday" means to derive pleasure from watching barbaric and gory entertainment.

Total Words Read _____
− Errors _____
= CWPM _____

Rocky Mountain States: Nature's Wonderland

0   The Rocky Mountains are the largest mountain range on the North
11   American continent. They stretch from north to south through the western
22   part of the United States to Canada. In the process, the Rockies cross six
36   states. These states are Colorado, Idaho, Montana, Nevada, Utah, and
46   Wyoming.
47   Several of America's national parks are located in the Rocky Mountain
58   states. The parks were created by the government to protect the nation's
70   natural resources. Yellowstone National Park is the oldest and largest
80   national park in the country. It is located mostly in northwestern Wyoming.
92   However, Yellowstone also spreads into neighboring southern Montana and
101   eastern Idaho. Yellowstone is famous for its many hot springs called "geysers."
113   One geyser named Old Faithful gushes every half-hour. Many animals like
125   elk, grizzly bears, moose, and bighorn sheep roam freely in Yellowstone.
136   Grand Teton National Park is located in northwestern Wyoming.
145   Almost three million people a year come to enjoy the beautiful snow-capped
158   Grand Teton Mountains. The 13,700-foot Grand Teton attracts many
168   mountain climbers and skiers.
172   Bryce Canyon National Park is located in southern Utah. The Piute
183   Indian word for the canyon means "red rocks standing like men in a bowl-
197   shaped canyon." The park's beautiful pink cliffs have been shaped by
208   erosion into unusual formations. Bryce Canyon National Park has some of
219   the nation's best air quality. It is an excellent spot for stargazing. Visitors
232   also enjoy panoramic views of three states. There are many hiking, skiing,
244   and horseback trails as well.
249

Total Words Read _____
− Errors _____
= CWPM _____

Archaeology: Digging for Buried Treasure

Archaeology is the study of earlier civilizations. Scientists who study early times are called archaeologists. Archaeologists look for artifact clues. Artifacts are manmade objects like pottery or tools. Artifacts provide important information. Sometimes artifacts are found by accident. Other times, artifacts are discovered by excavation. Artifacts can be preserved in sand and ice for many years. For example, treasures found in Egyptian tombs were buried in dry sand. They were found intact thousands of years later! When artifacts are found, they must be cleaned to remove sand or soil. Their exact position must be recorded. Artifacts are photographed so they can be studied. Artifacts provide important clues in helping to understand early humans. The archaeologists try to determine when and why the artifacts were important. They study artifacts to find out about the lives of the people who used them. Artifacts can provide clues as to what earlier people ate and drank. Artifacts can help determine whether ancient people traveled and if they played games.

Archaeologists in the United States look for Native American relics. These artifacts help them to learn facts about the Indians who lived before Columbus' time. Archaeologists in other parts of the world have found temples that were covered by a volcanic eruption more than a thousand years ago. Archaeology expeditions are ongoing all over the world. Sometimes governments pay for these expeditions. Sometimes colleges or private foundations absorb the cost. New discoveries are made all over the world every day!

Total Words Read _____

− Errors _____

= CWPM _____

Practice Passage 812

Oak Ridge: Secret City

Today, Oak Ridge is a small town located in the rolling hills of eastern Tennessee. During World War II, however, Oak Ridge was America's secret city. In 1942, Oak Ridge became a major site for the Manhattan Project. The Manhattan Project was created to produce the world's first atomic weapons. Scientists had discovered that large amounts of energy could split uranium atoms. This was called fission. Albert Einstein wrote to President Roosevelt discussing the potential of an atomic weapon to end the war. In 1942, it was discovered that there were three main methods for producing fissionable materials.

Oak Ridge was chosen as a government site for this important work. The city was isolated in the Black Oak Ridge Valley. However, it was accessible to highways and railroads. Electric power, water, and a labor supply were also available. Three production plants were built in Oak Ridge. These facilities were called by code names. The Y-12 plant separated uranium 235 from natural uranium. It used an electromagnetic process. The K-25 plant separated uranium 235 using a cheaper method. The third plant was called X-10. It was here that the Graphite Reactor was built. This reactor was the world's first nuclear reactor.

After World War II, the Manhattan Project was transferred to the Atomic Energy Commission. In 1948, X-10 became the Oak Ridge National Laboratory. In 1949, Oak Ridge was opened to the public. It is an unusual city in part because of its different beginnings. The city is populated with many highly educated and technically trained people. Oak Ridge is well known as a scientific center. It is also home to one of the nation's best rowing courses.

Total Words Read _____

− Errors _____

= CWPM _____

Practice Passage 813

Olympic Torchbearers: Keepers of the Flame

The lighting of an Olympic flame began thousands of years ago in ancient Greece. It is an Olympic tradition that continues today. The first Olympic flame was lit from the sun's rays in Olympia. The flame remained lit until the end of the Games. The ancient tradition of the Olympic flame was introduced in the modern Olympics at the Amsterdam Games in 1928. The Olympic flame symbolizes "the light of spirit, knowledge, and life."

The Olympic Torch Relay tradition also began in ancient Greece. The early Greeks would allow nothing, not even war, to interfere with their Olympic games. The Greeks called for a sacred truce before the start of the Olympics. They sent runners called "heralds of peace" to travel through Greece. These runners announced the start of the truce and invited people to come to the Olympic games. In the ancient Olympic games, the torch was lit at Olympia and then taken by relay to the city hosting the games. The Olympic Torch Relay tradition was introduced to the modern Olympics at the Berlin games in 1936. During the opening ceremony of the Olympic Games, the last runner in the relay carries the torch into the stadium. The torch is used to light the Olympic flame. The Olympic flame remains burning until it is extinguished during the closing ceremony.

Today, the Olympic flame is carried by thousands of torchbearers. Being selected as a torchbearer is a true honor. Torchbearers are nominated by friends, family members, or coworkers. Potential torchbearers are people who reflect the Olympic spirit. Often, torchbearers are ordinary people who have overcome personal challenges or who have inspired others.

Total Words Read _____
− Errors _____
= CWPM _____

The Cherokee Trail of Tears: 1828 to 1839

     The Trail of Tears was a sad event in American history. It took place from May of 1838 until March of 1839. During this time, 16,000 Cherokee people were made to leave their homes. They were forced to walk barefoot from southeastern Tennessee to Oklahoma. The weather conditions were terrible. It is believed that at least 4,000 Cherokee people died on the Trail of Tears.

     The Cherokee, as well as other Indian nations, had lived in North America for many years. As Europeans came to the United States to settle, many Native Americans were pushed off their land. This practice continued with the birth of the United States. The Native Americans gradually lost control of their lands for several reasons. First, the United States government did not view Native Americans as citizens. Therefore, the government did not grant them equal rights under the law. Another reason was that the government did not enforce treaties that protected Native American rights. The westward movement of settlers and the gold rush were other factors.

     In 1830, gold was discovered on Cherokee land in Tennessee. The United States government wanted these lands. That same year, the Indian Removal Act was passed by Congress. The government no longer suggested that the Native Americans move away from their homelands. Instead, the government ordered them to do so.

Total Words Read _____

− Errors _____

= CWPM _____

John James Audubon: A Natural Artist

John James was born on the island of Haiti in 1785. Because his father was French, he spent his early years in France. When John James was eighteen years old, his father sent him to oversee some lead mines he owned in southeastern Pennsylvania. He met his neighbor's daughter, Lucy Bakewell, in 1803. John and Lucy were married in 1808 and moved to Louisville, Kentucky, to open a general store with a business partner.

While John's partner took care of the business, John was busy drawing birds. He spent most of his days out in the woods looking for birds while Lucy raised their children. The general store failed, and it was the first of many of Audubon's businesses to fail. Since Audubon was in debt, he was arrested by the sheriff and put into debtor's prison in 1819. The sheriff took all of his belongings except for his portfolio of bird drawings, which he thought was worthless.

After he was out of jail, Audubon became a street artist, drawing "while you wait" portraits. He only worked in water paints and pastel chalks because he did not know how to paint in oils. Audubon began a journey to paint all of the birds in America, but he was unable to find a publisher to publish his book of bird paintings in this country. He went to Europe in 1826 and was able to get his book *Birds of America* published in 1827. He eventually became America's most famous wildlife artist. His work is still the standard on which contemporary wildlife artists are judged. The Audubon Society, a wildlife protection organization, is named after John James Audubon.

Practice Passage 816

Why Seven Wonders?

The first list of the seven wonders of the world was started during ancient times. Long ago, about two centuries before the birth of Christ, the most amazing buildings of the time were considered to be the seven wonders. The Great Pyramids of Egypt were the oldest in the original group. The pyramids are the only wonder still standing today.

The idea of "seven wonders" has continued through time. The number seven is thought to be special in many ways. For example, seven is a combination of the numbers three and four. Three and four are considered perfect numbers because of the way they form the perfect shapes of a triangle and a rectangle. The number seven is also found in the Bible, in philosophy, art, and in Chinese symbols. Examples of seven wonders are available across the "seven seas" and on the "seven continents"!

The ancient world had only one list of seven wonders. Today, however, there are so many wonders in our modern world that it would be impossible to choose only seven. Consequently, there are many different lists of the seven wonders, in a variety of areas. Some lists include examples of building design and artistic values. Other lists mention wonders of nature as well as science, invention, and medicine. Beautiful locations in the United States, such as the Grand Canyon and Yellowstone Park, have been included on lists of scenic wonders. Famous buildings, such as the Empire State Building and the Washington Monument, have been included on lists of buildings, along with the Eiffel Tower, the Leaning Tower of Pisa, and the Taj Mahal.

Total Words Read _____

− Errors _____

= CWPM _____

Level 8 Practice Passages

Practice Passage 817

Southwestern United States: The Mighty Four

The southwestern region of the United States has four states. They are Arizona, New Mexico, Oklahoma, and Texas. While small in number, the region is very large. For example, Texas is the largest state in the continental United States. The Southwest is a region with many mountains, deserts, and open land. Native Americans settled there thousands of years ago. When the Spanish arrived in 1500, they found established Indian villages. These Native Americans were living in apartment-like buildings called pueblos.

Oklahoma was the first southwest state to become part of the United States. Texas joined the union in 1845. New Mexico and Arizona were obtained as a result of the Mexican War in 1848. Today, many Native Americans live in the Southwest. More live in Oklahoma than in any other state in the United States. Arizona also has a large Native American population.

Today, the Southwest is the biggest producer of oil in the nation. Texas produces the most oil. Oklahoma and New Mexico are also big producers of oil. The southwestern states also support many large cattle ranches. Cowpokes work on these ranches and herd cattle by horseback. Arizona is home to America's most famous national feature, the Grand Canyon. This enormous canyon was created by a gorge of the Colorado River. The Grand Canyon stretches 227 miles across the northwest part of Arizona. People come from all over the world to see the beautiful layers of colored rock. Other natural landmarks found in Arizona are the Painted Desert and the Petrified Forest.

Total Words Read _____

− Errors _____

= CWPM _____

Pacific Coast: The Last Frontier

The Pacific Coast region is in the western United States. There are five states in this region. California, Oregon, and Washington are three of the states. They are also part of the continental United States. In fact, these adjoining states share a common coastline. They have two natural borders: the Pacific Ocean on the west and mountain ranges on the east.

The other two Pacific Coast states, Alaska and Hawaii, are separate. Alaska is a large peninsula in the far northwest corner of North America. It is completely separated from the continental United States by Canada. Hawaii is a chain of islands halfway across the Pacific Ocean.

Unlike states in the other United States regions, the Pacific Coast states are vastly different from one another. One big difference is in their geography. For example, Hawaii's lush tropical islands are in direct contrast to Alaska's frozen tundra and vast wilderness. The three other Pacific Coast states have striking, but different, landscapes. Another difference can be found in the residents. The region is home to a richly diverse population. In California, for example, Hispanics, Asians, and African Americans make up almost half of the population. One-sixth of the population of Alaska are Eskimos or Native American people. In Hawaii, there are many people of Asian and indigenous descent.

The Pacific Coast region is rich in natural resources. California grows much of the country's fruits and vegetables. Most of the timber in the United States comes from Washington and Oregon. Alaska has natural oil and gas. Hawaii grows much of the world's sugar cane and pineapple. Much diversity and many natural treasures can be found in the Pacific Coast region.

Graphite Reactor: The World's First Nuclear Reactor

     The Graphite Reactor is the oldest nuclear reactor in the world. It was built in only eleven months. It was part of the Manhattan Project. The Manhattan Project was a large World War II project. It was created to produce the world's first atomic weapons. The Graphite Reactor is located in Oak Ridge, Tennessee.

     In 1942, something important happened at the University of Chicago. It was a self-sustaining nuclear reaction. This event inspired the idea of the Graphite Reactor. At the Graphite Reactor, scientists made the first plutonium used to create a nuclear weapon. The Graphite Reactor became the model for other plutonium production reactors.

     After World War II, the Graphite Reactor began to make radioisotopes. Radioisotopes are used for military purposes. They are also used in science, medical, and technology programs. The Graphite Reactor became the world's major producer of nonmilitary radioisotopes. The reactor sent its first shipment of radioisotopes in 1946. It was sent to a special hospital in St. Louis, Missouri. The hospital was the Bernard Free Skin and Cancer Hospital. The Graphite Reactor was also used to research the effects of radiation on matter.

     The Graphite Reactor was used from 1943 to 1963. During those twenty years, it made many important contributions. The Graphite Reactor was named a National Historic Landmark in 1966. It was opened to the public in 1968. For many years, visitors enjoyed visiting the Graphite Reactor site. After September 11, 2001, however, access was closed for security reasons.

Total Words Read _____

− Errors _____

= CWPM _____

Practice Passage 820

Olympics: An Ancient Tradition

      Millions of people worldwide enjoy watching the Olympic games. In February 2002, the Winter Olympics were held in Salt Lake City, Utah. Many spectators may not have realized that these games originated thousands of years ago. The Olympics began in 776 B.C. when the ancient Greeks held a sporting competition. The first Olympic games consisted of only one event. It was a foot race in which only Greek men could participate. Later the Greeks added events such as the discus throw, horse and chariot races, and wrestling and boxing. The Olympics were just as important in ancient Greece as they are today. The ancient Greeks viewed the Olympics as so important that they allowed nothing to interfere with the every-four-year event.

      There are some differences between the ancient and current Olympics, however. The main difference is the actual purpose of the Olympics. In ancient Greece, the purpose of all public events, including the Olympics, was to honor the gods. So the ancient Olympics were actually religious celebrations. Today, however, the main purpose of the Olympics is to highlight the participating countries' athletic talent. The ancient games consisted of fewer events than current Olympic games. In Salt Lake City, the 17 days of Olympic games included all kinds of skiing, skating, ice hockey, and sled racing. Another difference between the ancient and present-day Olympics is the participants themselves. In ancient Greece, the Olympics were open only to Greek men. Today, of course, the Games are open to qualified men and women from around the world.

Total Words Read _____

− Errors _____

= CWPM _____

Level 8 Practice Passages

Automatic Word Lists

The *Automatic Word Lists* contain the most frequently encountered sight words in reading texts (Carroll, Davies, and Richman, 1971). These lists can be used to build fluency at the single-word level and to increase sight-word recognition. Struggling readers will benefit from additional fluency timings that focus on these high-frequency words.

Three to five times per week, have students who are reading below 40 cwpm work on their *Automatic Word Lists* instead of their *Practice Passages* during the timed *Six-Minute Solution* fluency practices.

During small group instruction, provide additional fluency practice with single words using the *Automatic Word Lists*.

Determining Which Automatic Word List to Use

To determine which *Automatic Word List* to use with a student, begin with *Automatic Words—Set 1* and move sequentially through the sets. Time the student for one minute on each set, beginning with *Set 1*. When the student reads less than 60 cwpm, stop. This is the set to use to build sight-word fluency. Have the student practice with the set until he or she reads 60 cwpm on two subsequent timings. Then move on to the next set.

Determining CWPM

Use the numbering on the left side of each set to quickly determine the total number of words read. Count the number of words that were errors. Subtract the number of words that were errors from the total number of words read in order to determine the cwpm (correct words per minute).

SET 1

Automatic Word List

0	the	of	and	to	a
5	in	that	is	was	he
10	for	it	with	as	his
15	on	be	at	by	I
20	this	had	not	are	but
25	the	of	and	to	a
30	in	that	is	was	he
35	for	it	with	as	his
40	on	be	at	by	I
45	this	had	not	are	but
50	the	of	and	to	a
55	in	that	is	was	he
60	for	it	with	as	his
65	on	be	at	by	I
70	this	had	not	are	but
75					

Total Words Read _____

− Errors _____

= CWPM _____

Automatic Word List

SET 2

0	from	or	have	an	they
5	which	one	you	were	her
10	all	she	there	would	their
15	we	him	been	has	when
20	who	will	more	no	if
25	from	or	have	an	they
30	which	one	you	were	her
35	all	she	there	would	their
40	we	him	been	has	when
45	who	will	more	no	if
50	from	or	have	an	they
55	which	one	you	were	her
60	all	she	there	would	their
65	we	him	been	has	when
70	who	will	more	no	if
75					

Total Words Read _____

− Errors _____

= CWPM _____

SET 3

Automatic Word List

0	out	so	said	what	up
5	its	about	into	than	them
10	can	only	other	new	some
15	time	could	these	two	may
20	then	do	first	any	my
25	out	so	said	what	up
30	its	about	into	than	them
35	can	only	other	new	some
40	time	could	these	two	may
45	then	do	first	any	my
50	out	so	said	what	up
55	its	about	into	than	them
60	can	only	other	new	some
65	time	could	these	two	may
70	then	do	first	any	my
75					

Total Words Read _____
- Errors _____
= CWPM _____

SET 4

Automatic Word List

0	now	such	like	our	over
5	man	me	even	most	made
10	after	also	did	many	before
15	must	through	back	years	where
20	much	your	way	well	down
25	now	such	like	our	over
30	man	me	even	most	made
35	after	also	did	many	before
40	must	through	back	years	where
45	much	your	way	well	down
50	now	such	like	our	over
55	man	me	even	most	made
60	after	also	did	many	before
65	must	through	back	years	where
70	much	your	way	well	down
75					

Total Words Read _____

− Errors _____

= CWPM _____

Automatic Word Lists

SET 5

Automatic Word List

0	should	because	each	just	those
5	people	Mr.	how	too	little
10	us	state	good	very	make
15	world	still	see	own	men
20	work	long	here	get	both
25	should	because	each	just	those
30	people	Mr.	how	too	little
35	us	state	good	very	make
40	world	still	see	own	men
45	work	long	here	get	both
50	should	because	each	just	those
55	people	Mr.	how	too	little
60	us	state	good	very	make
65	world	still	see	own	men
70	work	long	here	get	both
75					

Total Words Read _____

− Errors _____

= CWPM _____

SET 6

Automatic Word List

0	between	life	being	under	never
5	day	same	another	know	year
10	while	last	might	great	old
15	off	come	since	go	against
20	came	right	states	used	take
25	between	life	being	under	never
30	day	same	another	know	year
35	while	last	might	great	old
40	off	come	since	go	against
45	came	right	states	used	take
50	between	life	being	under	never
55	day	same	another	know	year
60	while	last	might	great	old
65	off	come	since	go	against
70	came	right	states	used	take
75					

Total Words Read _____
− Errors _____
= CWPM _____

SET 7

Automatic Word List

0	three	himself	few	house	use
5	during	without	again	place	American
10	around	however	home	small	found
15	Mrs.	thought	went	say	part
20	once	high	general	upon	school
25	three	himself	few	house	use
30	during	without	again	place	American
35	around	however	home	small	found
40	Mrs.	thought	went	say	part
45	once	high	general	upon	school
50	three	himself	few	house	use
55	during	without	again	place	American
60	around	however	home	small	found
65	Mrs.	thought	went	say	part
70	once	high	general	upon	school
75					

Total Words Read _____
− Errors _____
= CWPM _____

Automatic Word List

SET 8

0	every	don't	does	got	united
5	left	number	course	war	until
10	always	away	something	fact	water
15	though	less	public	put	think
20	almost	hand	enough	far	look
25	every	don't	does	got	united
30	left	number	course	war	until
35	always	away	something	fact	water
40	though	less	public	put	think
45	almost	hand	enough	far	look
50	every	don't	does	got	united
55	left	number	course	war	until
60	always	away	something	fact	water
65	though	less	public	put	think
70	almost	hand	enough	far	look
75					

Total Words Read _____
− Errors _____
= CWPM _____

SET 9

Automatic Word List

0	head	yet	government	system	set
5	better	told	nothing	night	end
10	why	didn't	know	eyes	find
15	going	look	asked	later	point
20	knew	city	next	program	business
25	head	yet	government	system	set
30	better	told	nothing	night	end
35	why	didn't	know	eyes	find
40	going	look	asked	later	point
45	knew	city	next	program	business
50	head	yet	government	system	set
55	better	told	nothing	night	end
60	why	didn't	know	eyes	find
65	going	look	asked	later	point
70	knew	city	next	program	business
75					

Total Words Read _____

− Errors _____

= CWPM _____

SET 10

Automatic Word List

0	give	group	toward	days	young
5	let	room	president	side	social
10	present	given	several	order	national
15	second	possible	rather	per	face
20	among	form	important	often	things
25	give	group	toward	days	young
30	let	room	president	side	social
35	present	given	several	order	national
40	second	possible	rather	per	face
45	among	form	important	often	things
50	give	group	toward	days	young
55	let	room	president	side	social
60	present	given	several	order	national
65	second	possible	rather	per	face
70	among	form	important	often	things
75					

Total Words Read _____

− Errors _____

= CWPM _____

Automatic Word Lists

SET 11

Automatic Word List

0	looked	early	white	John	case
5	become	large	need	big	four
10	within	fell	children	along	say
15	best	church	ever	least	power
20	development	thing	light	seemed	family
25	looked	early	white	John	case
30	become	large	need	big	four
35	within	fell	children	along	say
40	best	church	ever	least	power
45	development	thing	light	seemed	family
50	looked	early	white	John	case
55	become	large	need	big	four
60	within	fell	children	along	say
65	best	church	ever	least	power
70	development	thing	light	seemed	family
75					

Total Words Read _____

− Errors _____

= CWPM _____

SET 12

Automatic Word List

0	interest	want	members	others	mind
5	country	area	done	turned	although
10	open	God	service	problem	certain
15	kind	different	thus	began	door
20	help	means	sense	whole	matter
25	interest	want	members	others	mind
30	country	area	done	turned	although
35	open	God	service	problem	certain
40	kind	different	thus	began	door
45	help	means	sense	whole	matter
50	interest	want	members	others	mind
55	country	area	done	turned	although
60	open	God	service	problem	certain
65	kind	different	thus	began	door
70	help	means	sense	whole	matter
75					

Total Words Read _____
− Errors _____
= CWPM _____

Automatic Word Lists **227**

SET 13

Automatic Word List

0	perhaps	itself	York	it's	times
5	law	human	line	above	name
10	example	action	company	hands	local
15	show	whether	five	history	gave
20	today	either	act	feet	across
25	perhaps	itself	York	it's	times
30	law	human	line	above	name
35	example	action	company	hands	local
40	show	whether	five	history	gave
45	today	either	act	feet	across
50	perhaps	itself	York	it's	times
55	law	human	line	above	name
60	example	action	company	hands	local
65	show	whether	five	history	gave
70	today	either	act	feet	across
75					

Total Words Read _____
− Errors _____
= CWPM _____

SET 14

Automatic Word List

0	taken	past	quite	anything	seen
5	having	death	week	experience	body
10	word	half	really	field	am
15	car	words	already	themselves	I'm
20	information	tell	together	college	shall
25	taken	past	quite	anything	seen
30	having	death	week	experience	body
35	word	half	really	field	am
40	car	words	already	themselves	I'm
45	information	tell	together	college	shall
50	taken	past	quite	anything	seen
55	having	death	week	experience	body
60	word	half	really	field	am
65	car	words	already	themselves	I'm
70	information	tell	together	college	shall
75					

Total Words Read _____

− Errors _____

= CWPM _____

Automatic Word Lists

SET 15

Automatic Word List

0	money	period	held	keep	sure
5	real	probably	free	seems	political
10	cannot	behind	Miss	question	air
15	office	making	brought	whose	special
20	major	heard	problems	federal	became
25	money	period	held	keep	sure
30	real	probably	free	seems	political
35	cannot	behind	Miss	question	air
40	office	making	brought	whose	special
45	major	heard	problems	federal	became
50	money	period	held	keep	sure
55	real	probably	free	seems	political
60	cannot	behind	Miss	question	air
65	office	making	brought	whose	special
70	major	heard	problems	federal	became
75					

Total Words Read _____

− Errors _____

= CWPM _____

SET 16

Automatic Word List

0	study	ago	moment	available	known
5	result	street	economic	boy	position
10	reason	change	south	board	individual
15	job	areas	society	west	close
20	turn	love	community	true	court
25	study	ago	moment	available	known
30	result	street	economic	boy	position
35	reason	change	south	board	individual
40	job	areas	society	west	close
45	turn	love	community	true	court
50	study	ago	moment	available	known
55	result	street	economic	boy	position
60	reason	change	south	board	individual
65	job	areas	society	west	close
70	turn	love	community	true	court
75					

Total Words Read _____

− Errors _____

= CWPM _____

Automatic Word Lists **231**

SET 17

Automatic Word List

0	force	full	course	seem	wife
5	future	age	wanted	department	voice
10	center	woman	control	common	policy
15	necessary	following	front	sometimes	six
20	girl	clear	further	land	run
25	force	full	course	seem	wife
30	future	age	wanted	department	voice
35	center	woman	control	common	policy
40	necessary	following	front	sometimes	six
45	girl	clear	further	land	run
50	force	full	course	seem	wife
55	future	age	wanted	department	voice
60	center	woman	control	common	policy
65	necessary	following	front	sometimes	six
70	girl	clear	further	land	run
75					

Total Words Read _____
− Errors _____
= CWPM _____

SET 18

Automatic Word List

0	students	provide	feel	party	able
5	mother	music	education	university	child
10	effect	level	stood	military	town
15	short	morning	total	outside	rate
20	figure	class	art	century	Washington
25	students	provide	feel	party	able
30	mother	music	education	university	child
35	effect	level	stood	military	town
40	short	morning	total	outside	rate
45	figure	class	art	century	Washington
50	students	provide	feel	party	able
55	mother	music	education	university	child
60	effect	level	stood	military	town
65	short	morning	total	outside	rate
70	figure	class	art	century	Washington
75					

Total Words Read _____

− Errors _____

= CWPM _____

Automatic Word Lists **233**

SET 19

Automatic Word List

0	north	usually	plan	leave	therefore
5	evidence	too	million	sound	black
10	strong	hard	various	says	believe
15	type	value	play	surface	soon
20	mean	near	lines	table	peace
25	north	usually	plan	leave	therefore
30	evidence	too	million	sound	black
35	strong	hard	various	says	believe
40	type	value	play	surface	soon
45	mean	near	lines	table	peace
50	north	usually	plan	leave	therefore
55	evidence	too	million	sound	black
60	strong	hard	various	says	believe
65	type	value	play	surface	soon
70	mean	near	lines	table	peace
75					

Total Words Read _____
− Errors _____
= CWPM _____

SET 20

Automatic Word List

0	modern	tax	road	red	book
5	personal	process	situation	minutes	increases
10	schools	idea	English	alone	women
15	gone	nor	living	months	America
20	started	longer	Dr.	cut	finally
25	modern	tax	road	red	book
30	personal	process	situation	minutes	increases
35	schools	idea	English	alone	women
40	gone	nor	living	months	America
45	started	longer	Dr.	cut	finally
50	modern	tax	road	red	book
55	personal	process	situation	minutes	increases
60	schools	idea	English	alone	women
65	gone	nor	living	months	America
70	started	longer	Dr.	cut	finally
75					

Total Words Read _____
− Errors _____
= CWPM _____

Automatic Word Lists **235**

SET 21

Automatic Word List

0	third	secretary	nature	private	section
5	greater	call	fire	expected	needed
10	that's	kept	ground	view	values
15	everything	pressure	dark	basis	space
20	east	father	required	union	spirit
25	third	secretary	nature	private	section
30	greater	call	fire	expected	needed
35	that's	kept	ground	view	values
40	everything	pressure	dark	basis	space
45	east	father	required	union	spirit
50	third	secretary	nature	private	section
55	greater	call	fire	expected	needed
60	that's	kept	ground	view	values
65	everything	pressure	dark	basis	space
70	east	father	required	union	spirit
75					

Total Words Read _____
− Errors _____
= CWPM _____

SET 22

Automatic Word List

0	except	complete	wrote	I'll	moved
5	support	return	conditions	recent	attention
10	late	particular	nations	hope	live
15	costs	else	brown	taking	couldn't
20	hours	person	forces	beyond	report
25	except	complete	wrote	I'll	moved
30	support	return	conditions	recent	attention
35	late	particular	nations	hope	live
40	costs	else	brown	taking	couldn't
45	hours	person	forces	beyond	report
50	except	complete	wrote	I'll	moved
55	support	return	conditions	recent	attention
60	late	particular	nations	hope	live
65	costs	else	brown	taking	couldn't
70	hours	person	forces	beyond	report
75					

Total Words Read _____
− Errors _____
= CWPM _____

Automatic Word Lists

SET 23

Automatic Word List

0	coming	inside	dead	low	stage
5	material	read	instead	lost	St.
10	heart	looking	miles	data	added
15	pay	amount	followed	feeling	single
20	makes	research	including	basic	hundred
25	coming	inside	dead	low	stage
30	material	read	instead	lost	St.
35	heart	looking	miles	data	added
40	pay	amount	followed	feeling	single
45	makes	research	including	basic	hundred
50	coming	inside	dead	low	stage
55	material	read	instead	lost	St.
60	heart	looking	miles	data	added
65	pay	amount	followed	feeling	single
70	makes	research	including	basic	hundred
75					

Total Words Read _____
- Errors _____
= CWPM _____

SET 24

Automatic Word List

0	move	industry	cold	developed	tried
5	simply	hold	can't	reached	committee
10	island	defense	equipment	son	actually
15	shown	religious	ten	river	getting
20	central	beginning	sort	received	doing
25	move	industry	cold	developed	tried
30	simply	hold	can't	reached	committee
35	island	defense	equipment	son	actually
40	shown	religious	ten	river	getting
45	central	beginning	sort	received	doing
50	move	industry	cold	developed	tried
55	simply	hold	can't	reached	committee
60	island	defense	equipment	son	actually
65	shown	religious	ten	river	getting
70	central	beginning	sort	received	doing
75					

Total Words Read _____

− Errors _____

= CWPM _____

SET 25

Automatic Word List

0	terms	trying	friends	rest	medical
5	care	especially	picture	indeed	administration
10	fine	subject	higher	difficult	simple
15	range	building	wall	meeting	walked
20	cent	floor	foreign	bring	similar
25	terms	trying	friends	rest	medical
30	care	especially	picture	indeed	administration
35	fine	subject	higher	difficult	simple
40	range	building	wall	meeting	walked
45	cent	floor	foreign	bring	similar
50	terms	trying	friends	rest	medical
55	care	especially	picture	indeed	administration
60	fine	subject	higher	difficult	simple
65	range	building	wall	meeting	walked
70	cent	floor	foreign	bring	similar
75					

Total Words Read _____

− Errors _____

= CWPM _____

Appendix

Fluency Assessment Report

STUDENT NAME: _____   GRADE: _____

TEACHER: _____   DATE: _____

Dear Parent,

Fluency training is an important part of our language arts program. We assess students _____ times a year and report the scores as correct words per minute (cwpm). Reading smoothly, efficiently, and accurately is a focus of our reading program. We practice our reading fluency skills in many ways. By the time students reach the fourth grade, they should be able to read at least 100 words per minute orally and their reading rates should increase every year. You can use this figure as a yardstick to measure your child's oral reading fluency rate.

Date	1 Timing Correct Words per Minute	Date	2 Timing Correct Words per Minute	Gain in Correct Words per Minute	Date	3 Timing Correct Words per Minute	Gain in Correct Words per Minute	Percent of Improvement During the Entire Year

242   Appendix

©2004 Sopris West Educational Services. Purchaser has permission to photocopy this page for classroom use only.

Initial Assessment Record

TEACHER: _____

CLASS: _____ DATE: _____

STUDENT NAME	ASSESSMENT 1—ORAL READING RATE (CWPM)	ASSESSMENT 2—INSTRUCTIONAL READING LEVEL

Rank students according to oral reading rate and then instructional reading level.

Fluency Record

NAME: _____ CLASS: _____

PASSAGE NUMBER: _____

PARTNER: _____ DATE: _____

PASSAGE #	DATE	CWPM	DATE	CWPM	DATE	CWPM	DATE	CWPM	DATE	CWPM

CWPM = correct words per minute

Fluency Graph 1

NAME: _____ CLASS: _____

PARTNER: _____ DATE: _____

CORRECT WORDS PER MINUTE

200
195
190
185
180
175
170
165
160
155
150
145
140
135
130
125
120
115
110
105
100
95
90
85
80
75
70
65
60
55
50
45
40
35
30
25
20
15
10
5

DATE

PASSAGE NUMBER

Appendix **245**

Fluency Graph 2

NAME: _____ CLASS: _____

PARTNER: _____ DATE: _____

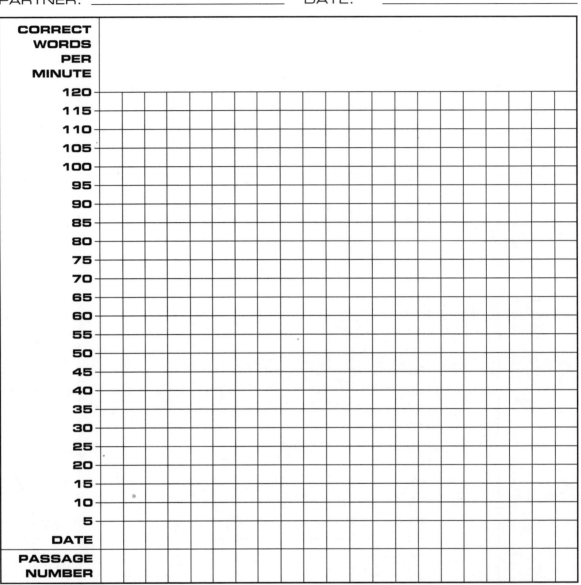

Fluency Graph 3

NAME: _____ CLASS: _____

PARTNER: _____ DATE: _____

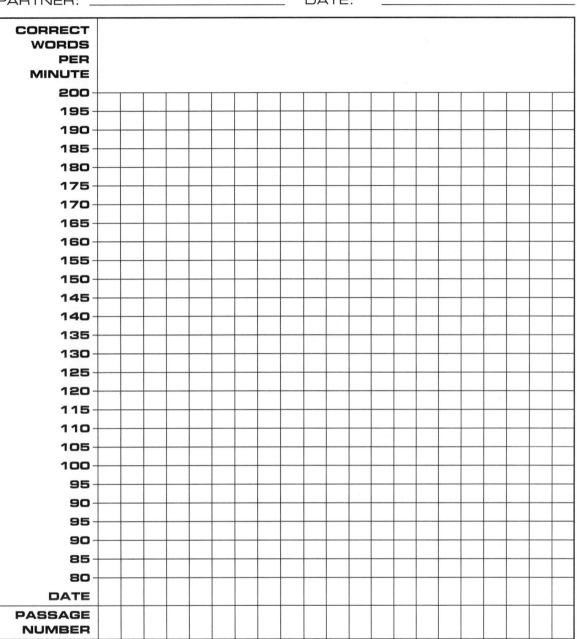

Appendix **247**

San Diego Quick Assessment of Reading Ability

Directions: This is an individually administered sight-word reading assessment. Because this is a measure of sight-word knowledge, students need to recognize the words very quickly. Give a copy of the Student Form to the student to read. Choose a word list that is two-to-three grade levels below the student's current grade level as the starting point. Ask the student to read each word aloud. Keep the student moving down the lists. Do not allow more than three to five seconds on any word. Rather, tell the student to go on to the next word. Mark the word skipped as incorrect. Stop the assessment when the student has missed three or more words in a list. Record the highest grade level for each of the three levels (independent, instructional, and frustration) in the Errors & Reading Levels table when testing is completed.

ERRORS & READING LEVELS			
Student Name	**Reading Level**		
	Independent (1 error)	Instructional (2 errors)	Frustration (3+ errors)

San Diego Quick Assessment of Reading Ability

Teacher Record

NAME: _____ DATE: _____

Record the highest grade level for each:

INDEPENDENT _____ INSTRUCTIONAL _____ FRUSTRATION _____

Preprimer	**Grade Three**	**Grade Seven**	**Grade Eleven**
see	city	amber	galore
play	middle	dominion	rotunda
me	moment	sundry	capitalism
at	frightened	capillary	prevaricate
run	exclaimed	impetuous	visible
go	several	blight	exonerate
and	lonely	wrest	superannuate
look	drew	enumerate	luxuriate
can	since	daunted	piebald
here	straight	condescend	crunch

Primer	**Grade Four**	**Grade Eight**	
you	decided	capacious	
come	served	limitation	
not	amazed	pretext	
with	silent	intrigue	
jump	wrecked	delusion	
help	improved	immaculate	
is	certainly	ascent	
work	entered	acrid	
are	realized	binocular	
this	interrupted	embankment	

Grade One	**Grade Five**	**Grade Nine**	
road	scanty	conscientious	
live	business	isolation	
thank	develop	molecule	
when	considered	ritual	
bigger	discussed	momentous	
how	behaved	vulnerable	
always	splendid	kinship	
night	acquainted	conservatism	
spring	escaped	jaunty	
today	grim	inventive	

Grade Two	**Grade Six**	**Grade Ten**	
our	bridge	zany	
please	commercial	jerkin	
myself	abolish	nausea	
town	trucker	gratuitous	
early	apparatus	linear	
send	elementary	inept	
wide	comment	legality	
believe	necessity	aspen	
quietly	gallery	amnesty	
carefully	relativity	barometer	

From "The Graded Word List: Quick Gauge of Reading Ability" by Margaret LaPray, Helen Ross, and Raman Royal, in *Journal of Reading, 12,* 305–307 (January, 1969) Copyright © by Margaret LaPray and the International Reading Association. All rights reserved. Reprinted with permission.

San Diego Quick Assessment of Reading Ability

Student Form

see	exclaimed	daunted
play	several	condescend
me	lonely	capacious
at	drew	limitation
run	since	pretext
go	straight	intrigue
and	decided	delusion
look	served	immaculate
can	amazed	ascent
here	silent	acrid
you	wrecked	binocular
come	improved	embankment
not	certainly	conscientious
with	entered	isolation
jump	realized	molecule
help	interrupted	ritual
is	scanty	momentous
work	business	vulnerable
are	develop	kinship
this	considered	conservatism
road	discussed	jaunty
live	behaved	inventive
thank	splendid	zany
when	acquainted	jerkin
bigger	escaped	nausea
how	grim	gratuitous
always	bridge	linear
night	commercial	inept
spring	abolish	legality
today	trucker	aspen
our	apparatus	amnesty
please	elementary	barometer
myself	comment	galore
town	necessity	rotunda
early	gallery	capitalism
send	relativity	prevaricate
wide	amber	visible
believe	dominion	exonerate
quietly	sundry	superannuate
carefully	capillary	luxuriate
city	impetuous	piebald
middle	blight	crunch
moment	wrest	
frightened	enumerate	

Three Six-Minute Solution Field Tests

Field Test I

A description of the *Six-Minute Solution* intervention program was published as "Working with Words: A Summer Reading Intervention Program" (Adams, Brown, and Van Zant, 2000) and as "Summer Reading Intervention Program Prepares Fifth Grade Students for Middle School Reading Challenges" (Adams, Brown, and Van Zant, 1999). *Six-Minute Solution* is also featured as part of "Teaching Reading in Every Classroom," an online staff development program, at the San Diego County Office of Education, San Diego, California.

Location

In the summer of 1999, the authors developed a summer reading intervention program for at-risk middle school readers at Meadowbrook Middle School (in Poway, California, a town 20 miles north of downtown San Diego). The *Six-Minute Solution* model was a critical component. Meadowbrook, built in 1964, is the oldest middle school in the Poway Unified School District. The 1,515 students represent a rich diversity of cultural, ethnic, linguistic, and religious backgrounds. Thirty-one percent of the students are non-Anglo, the largest ethnic group being Filipino. Of the 1,515 students, 108 students speak a language other than English in their homes.

Participants

Fifty-two students (who were reading at least two years below grade level) were selected to attend this 24-day summer school intervention program. Additionally, 30 of the 52 intervention program participants (58 percent) had previously been identified as eligible for special education services or English Language Learner (ELL) support. Students were in this reading class two hours a day, Monday through Friday. The teacher-student ratio was 1 to 26 for each class. Students were divided into two homogeneous classes based on instructional levels.

Procedure

Using the assessment procedures described in this book, students were assigned fluency partners. These student partners practiced fluency daily—either with *Automatic Word Lists* or with *Practice Passages* at their instructional reading levels. Students also were taught a multisyllabic word decoding strategy using the *REWARDS: Reading Excellence, Word Attack, and Rate Development Strategies* program (Archer, Gleason, and Vachon; 2000). Students received direct instruction in reading comprehension strategies and in paragraph writing. Additionally, students participated in "novel partnerships" in which they read trade books to each other in five-minute segments and practiced oral comprehension strategies.

Reading gains recorded by the summer school intervention students were outstanding in many cases. Pre-assessment fluency scores on a sixth-grade passage ranged from a low of 40 correct words per minute (cwpm) to a high of 136 cwpm. Post-assessment rates ranged from a low of 61 cwpm to a high of 195 cwpm. The average reading fluency gain was 36 percent.

Comprehension gains were also considerable. Pre-assessment reading comprehension scores ranged from a lexile level of 260 (first grade) to a high of 905 (fifth grade). Post-assessment scores ranged from a low of 395 (second grade) to a high of 1050 (sixth grade). One class gained an average of 166 lexile points (a gain equivalent to between one and two grade years). The second class gained an average of 133 lexile points (a one-half to one-year grade equivalent). As measured by pre- and post-lexile readability scales, the overall growth in reading comprehension was 26 percent.

Note: A **lexile** is a measure of the reading difficulty of a text. It is a number on a scale representing the semantic difficulty and the syntactic complexity of the text. The lexile scale ranges from 0 to 2000 and can be correlated to a text's readability. Instead of assigning a readability level to a text such as "4.2" or "6.7," signifying a grade level, the lexile assigns a number such as 853. This lexile means that the text is on a fifth-to-sixth-grade reading level. When an assessment reports a score as a lexile, the lexile reading score can then be matched to a list of titles that fall within the lexile reading range. The Lexile Framework Web Site, *www.lexile.com,* offers a wealth of information about this reading tool.

Field Test II

Location

In the 2000–2001 school year, teachers from Dana Middle School in the San Diego Unified School District, San Diego, California, were trained in the *Six-Minute Solution* fluency-partner model as part of their participation in the "Teaching Reading in Every Classroom" online staff development program. Dana Middle School has 864 fifth- and sixth-graders. Fifty percent of the student body is Caucasian. Twenty-nine percent are Hispanic, and nine percent are African-American. A Title I school, Dana Middle School is one in which 48 percent of students qualify for the free and reduced lunch program. Dana Middle School identified its lowest performing readers by examining their Scholastic Achievement Test (Harcourt, 2001) and Stanford Diagnostic Reading Test (Bjorn and Gardner, 2001) scores from the 1999–2000 school year.

Participants and Procedure

Of the 864 students who attend Dana Middle School, 120 were placed into six groups of 20 students each. They formed six sections of an elective class called Dana Readers' Club (DRC). These students received one additional hour of reading support, four days a week. Students were paired with partners and practiced reading both instructionally appropriate passages and sight words using the *Six-Minute Solution* model. Students received additional instruction in reading multisyllabic words and specific skill instruction in the form of mini-lessons and guided practice.

Data was collected on 92 students. Students in quartile one made an average of 1.52 years growth during the span of one school year. Students in the other groups did not make as impressive growth, but 91 of the 92 students (99 percent) demonstrated measurable growth in oral-reading fluency, with 61 of the 92 students (66 percent) evidencing a 25 percent or better increase in their oral reading rate. Moreover, 42 of the 92 students' (46 percent) post-reading-fluency scores placed them within the average oral-reading-fluency range for sixth-grade students. The teachers who participated in this project became convinced of the power of repeated readings, timed sight words, and word study. Anecdotal reports by teachers and students suggest that students spent more time actively reading, showed more pleasure in reading, and were more likely to perceive themselves as readers.

Field Test III

Location

In the 2001–2002 school year, the *Six-Minute Solution* was implemented in two upper-grade classrooms at Los Penasquitos Elementary School over a three-month period. Los Penasquitos Elementary School is in the Poway Unified School District in California. At Los Penasquitos, there are 635 students, representing 21 languages, in grades kindergarten through five. Los Penasquitos is a Title I school, with 41 percent of students qualifying for the free and reduced lunch program.

Participants and Procedure

The *Six-Minute Solution* was implemented in two classrooms: a heterogeneous fourth-grade classroom of 31 students and a combined fourth–fifth grade class in the Los Penasquitos Academy. In the fourth-grade classroom, the smallest gain was 18 percent and the largest gain was 91 percent. The average gain in oral reading fluency for the class was 38 percent. Twenty-six of the 31 students (84 percent) increased their oral reading rates by more than 25 percent. In the fourth–fifth grade Academy class, students attend school 48 percent more hours than do students in traditional classes (1600 hours vs. 1080 hours). Both a longer school day and a longer school year give Academy students the extended time necessary to acquire the knowledge, skills, and character traits that are essential for success in rigorous high school programs, and for admission to competitive universities. In the fourth–fifth grade Academy classroom, 24 of the 25 students (95 percent) demonstrated a significant gain in oral reading fluency as measured by a comparison of pre- and post-cwpm scores on grade-level passages.

References

Adams, G., Brown, S., and Van Zant, S. 2000. Working with words: A summer reading intervention program. *Principal,* 80 (1): 59–60. Alexandria, VA: National Association of Elementary School Principals (NAESP).

Adams, G., Brown, S., and Van Zant, S. 1999. Summer reading intervention program prepares fifth grade students for middle school reading challenges. *Educational Research Service Successful School Practices,* 22 (1): 6–8. Arlington, VA: Educational Research Service.

Allington, R. L. 1983. Fluency: The neglected reading goal in reading instruction. *The Reading Teacher,* 36:556–561.

Allington, R. L. 1977. If they don't read much, how are they ever gonna get good? *Journal of Reading,* 21:57–61.

Archer, A. L. and Gleason, M. M. 2002. *Skills for school success series.* North Billerica, MA: Curriculum Associates, Inc.

Archer, A. L., Gleason, M. M., and Vachon, V. L. 2000. *REWARDS: Reading excellence, word attack, and rate development strategies.* Longmont, CO: Sopris West Educational Services.

Carnine, D., Silbert, J., and Kameenui, E. J. 1997. *Direct instruction reading* (3rd ed.). Upper Saddle River, N.J.: Prentice-Hall.

Carpenter, P. A. and Just, M. A. (1983). What your eyes do while your mind is reading. In K. Rayner, ed., *Eye movements in reading: Perceptual and language processes* (pp. 275–307). New York: Academic Press.

Carroll, J., Davies, P., and Richman, B. 1971. *The American Heritage word frequency book.* Boston, MA: Houghton Mifflin Co, American Heritage Publishing Co.

Cunningham, A. E. and Stanovich, K. E. 1998. What reading does for the mind. *American Educator,* 22 (1–2):8–15.

Dowhower, S. L. 1987. Effects of repeated reading on second-grade transitional readers' fluency and comprehension. *Reading Research Quarterly,* 22:389–406

Dowhower, S. L. 1994. Repeated reading revisited: Research into practice. *Reading and Writing Quarterly,* 10:343–358.

Farstrup, A. E. and Samuels, S. J., Eds. 2002. *What research has to say about reading instruction* (3rd ed). Newark, DE: International Reading Association.

Fuchs, L. S., Fuchs, D., Kazlan, S., and Allen, S. 1999. Effects of peer-assisted learning strategies in reading with and without training in elaborated help giving. *Elementary School Journal,* 99 (3):201–220.

Greenwood, C. R., Delquadri, J. C., and Hall, R. V. 1989. Longitudinal effects of Classwide Peer Tutoring. *Journal of Educational Psychology,* 81, 371–383.

Harcourt, Inc: 2001. Scholastic achievement test (SAT-9) test series (9th ed.): Author.

Hasbrouck, J. E. and Tindal, G. 1992. Curriculum-based oral reading fluency norms for students in grades 2 through 5. *Teaching Exceptional Children,* 24 (3):41–44.

Karlsen, B. and Gardner, E. F. 2001. *Stanford diagnostic reading test* (4th ed.). San Antonio, TX: Harcourt, Inc.

LaPray, M., Ross, H., Royal, R. The graded word list: Quick gauge of reading ability. *Journal of Reading, 12,* 305–307. International Reading Association.

Levy, B. A. 2001. Moving the bottom: Improving reading fluency. In M. Wolf, ed., *Dyslexia, fluency, and the brain.* Parkton, MD: York Press.

Levy, B. A., Nicholls, A., and Kroshen, D. 1993. Repeated readings: Process benefits for good and poor readers. *Journal of Experimental Child Psychology,* 56:303–327.

MacGinitie, W., MacGinitie, R., Maria, K., and Dreyer, L. 2003. Gates MacGinitie reading tests. Itasca, IL: Riverside Publishing Company.

McLeod, J. and McLeod R. 1999. CORE (Consortium on Reading Excellence, Inc.). Novato, CA: Arena Press.

Meyer, M. S. and Felton, R. H. 1999. Repeated reading to enhanced fluency: Old approaches and new directions. *Annals of Dyslexia,* 49:263–306.

Mercer, C. D., Campbell, K. U., Miller, M. D., Mercer, K. D., and Lane, H. B. 2001. Effects of a reading fluency intervention for middle schoolers with specific learning disabilities. *Learning Disabilities Research and Practice,* 15:179–189.

Moats, L. C. 2001. When older kids can't read. *Educational Leadership Report.* March, 2001.

National Institute of Child Health and Human Development. 2000. Chapter 3: Fluency. In Report of the National Reading Panel: Teaching children to read: An evidence based assessment of the scientific research literature on reading and its implications for reading instruction. NIH Publication No. 00-4754. Washington, DC: U.S. Government Printing Office.

Pinnell, G. S., Piluski, J. J., Wixson, K. K. Campbell, J. R., Gough, P. B., and Beatty, A. S. 1995. *Listening to children read aloud: Data from NAEP's Integrated Reading Performance Record (IRPR) at grade 4.* Report No. 23-FR-04. Washington, DC: National Center for Education Statistics, Office of Educational Research and Improvement, U.S. Department of Education.

Rosenshine, B. and Meister, C. 1994. Reciprocal teaching: A review of research. *Review of Educational Research,* 64, 479–530.

Samuels, S. J. 1979. The method of repeated readings. *The Reading Teacher,* 32:403–408.

Scholastic, Inc. 2003. Scholastic reading inventory (SRI). New York: Author.

Shapiro, E. S. 1996. *Academic skills problems: Direct assessment and intervention* (2nd ed.). New York: Guilford Press.

Stanovich, K. E. 1990. Concepts in developmental theories of reading skill: Cognitive resources, automaticity, and modularity. *Developmental Review,* 10:72–100.

Stanovich, K. E. 1986. Matthews effect in reading: Some consequences of individual differences in the acquisition of literacy. *Reading Research Quarterly,* 21, 360–407.

Stevens, R. J., Madden, N. A., Slavin, R. E., and Famish, A. M. 1987. Cooperative integrated reading and composition: Two field experiments. *Reading Research Quarterly,* 22, 433–454.

Stieglitz, E. 2002. Stieglitz informal reading inventory: Assessing reading behaviors from emergent to advanced levels. Boston, MA: Allyn & Bacon.

Torgensen, J. K., Rashotte, C. A., and Alexander, A. 2001. Principles of fluency instruction in reading: Relationships with established empirical outcomes. In M. Wolf, ed., *Dyslexia, Fluency, and the Brain.* Parkton, MD: York Press.

Topping, K. 1987. Paired reading: A powerful techniques for parent use. *The Reading Teacher,* 40:608–614.

Wolf, M. 2001. *Dyslexia, fluency, and the brain.* Parkton, MD: York Press.

Woodcock, R. W. 2000. *Woodcock reading mastery test.* Circle Pines, MN: American Guidance Service Publishing.